Entering StartUpLand

Entering StartUpLand

An Essential Guide to Finding the Right Job

Jeffrey Bussgang

HARVARD BUSINESS REVIEW PRESS

Boston, Massachusetts

Library-of-Congress Cataloging-in-Publication Data

Names: Bussgang, Jeffrey, author.
Title: Entering Startupland : an essential guide to finding the right job /
    By Jeffrey Bussgang.
Description: Boston, Massachusetts : Harvard Business Review Press, [2017]
Identifiers: LCCN 2017017595 | ISBN 9781633693845 (hardcover : alk. paper)
Subjects: LCSH: New business enterprises. | Work environment. | Job hunting.
Classification: LCC HD62.5 .B875 2017 | DDC 658.1/1023--dc23 LC record available at https://lccn.loc.gov/2017017595

For Jackie, JJ, and Jonah.
May whatever land they
choose be open to them.

Contents

1. Introduction: Entering StartUpLand

Sitting on a shelf in my office is a 1990 vintage bottle of Dom Perignón. It was given to me by a strategy consulting firm in celebration of its offer to rejoin it after I completed business school. It remains unopened. Instead, I show the bottle to my students every year and tell them my personal story in hopes of inspiring them to enter StartUpLand.

What's that story?

I was you.

Twenty years ago, I was the audience for this book.

I graduated from college in 1991. After college, I went to work for The Boston Consulting Group (BCG), an amazing place that allowed me to learn about business and strategy at a very young age. A few years later, when I was admitted to business school, BCG offered to pay for school if I returned to work there. A lucrative offer to go into management consulting, return to a prestigious firm where I was comfortable, have business school paid for in full, and that bottle of Dom. Easy choice, right?

I turned them down.

My thinking was a little bit irrational and a little bit rational. The irrational side was that I was passionate about the internet and startups and knew I should follow my passion. I knew I would not forgive myself if I made a decision to compromise just for the money and the ease of fitting into a well-defined job and well-trodden career path. As I considered joining StartUpLand, I could feel my adrenalin pumping just thinking about leaping into the unknown.

For the rational part of the decision, even though I knew the consulting offer was far more lucrative and included tuition reimbursement, I thought, *Look, I'm young and don't yet have kids or a mortgage to worry about. I'm in a position where I can take some risk.* I felt, in the grand scheme of things, I should resist charting my course based on a short-term financial opportunity.

It was a tough decision. Many of my classmates said, "What are you doing? You're crazy!" It was like a *Far Side* cartoon where the penguins all go one way and there's one that goes the other way. But I had to go the other way.

So, as my classmates were rushing off to high-paying, high-powered jobs on Wall Street and at consulting firms, I hustled around town and networked my way into a Series A startup.[*] I joined as a product manager, making $65,000 per year—lower than my salary before entering business school.

The startup was called Open Market. It provided infrastructure for payments on the internet. It was the original, secure e-commerce platform back in the mid-1990s. The first shopping cart was created by our company. We invented (and patented) secure credit card transactions over the web.

Because of our early stage and ever-changing market, the place was bedlam. Browsers were just becoming popular, and the internet was in the earliest stages of development. It was a land grab. Open Market had thirty employees—maybe twenty of whom were engineers—and we were simultaneously working on ten products. It was like flying the plane while trying to build the engine at the same time. It was chaotic but thrilling. One of the big things I had

---

[*]Series A refers to a company's first round of significant funding and is typically led by a venture capital firm.

to learn to do was navigate in a world of tremendous uncertainty. Fortunately, we had a successful run. The company went public in 1996, only a year after I joined, and we eventually achieved a peak market capitalization of over $2 billion.

Because a startup is so small and dynamic, it gives great opportunity for personal and professional growth. For instance, during my five years at Open Market, I had the opportunity to run nearly every function in the company (e.g., marketing, product, professional services). I was hooked on StartUpLand and later cofounded another company, Upromise, where we were also lucky enough to have a successful run and built a valuable business that later sold for hundreds of millions of dollars.

Both of those companies were backed by several venture capital firms. One of those firms had two partners who were contemporaries and became good friends. Eventually, they decided to leave their firm, and fifteen years ago, we formed Flybridge Capital Partners, an early-stage venture capital firm with offices in Boston and New York City.

Along with my day job of investing in startups through Flybridge, I teach an entrepreneurship course for MBAs at Harvard Business School called Launching Technology Ventures. In both my capacities as a professor and venture capitalist, I am immersed in StartUpLand—I live, breath, eat, and sleep startups every day. And I love it. I'm still drawn to the excitement. It's a disease, I swear. Every startup still feels like a pioneer embarking on a new adventure.

Which brings me back to you and that bottle of Dom on my desk.

Why I Wrote This Book: Joiners

There are many, many books for founders, providing them with advice on how to raise money, build their companies, and live their lives. In fact, I wrote one of them—a book called *Mastering the*

VC Game, which is targeted at helping founders raise capital and grow their startup.

But there are very few books for *joiners*: the brave folks who want to join startups and figure out the best entry point. Employees number two through two thousand who work alongside the founders to take the original idea and do the hard work to actually create a company.

From the outside, startups seem confusing and murky. They seem chaotic—that there's no order to them. Because it lacks order, it is hard to figure out the best way to approach StartUpLand, know what the jobs are to be done, and figure out the best ways to explore and exploit professional opportunities. In contrast, the traditional business world is highly structured and organized, with centuries of organizational history and well-laid-out career paths.

I can't tell you how much time I've spent in my office talking to students about how to get into the startup world. And not just young professionals; interest in joining startups cuts across all ages and stages of careers. I have had many meetings with lawyers, doctors, scientists, professors, and experienced professionals who are intrigued by the magic that StartUpLand represents. In these conversations, I found myself giving the same advice over and over again. I tried to capture it in teaching notes and blog posts, then finally decided to put it all into a book, because clearly the information isn't widely available to those interested in entering StartUpLand.

In my fifteen years as a venture capitalist, I have invested in over a hundred startups. Through that work, I have developed a holistic view of company building and the elements required to do it. I work closely with founders as an investor and board member; my job is to coach them on building the company from scratch. From the embryonic stages through the more mature growth stage, I advise startups on how to stand up departments like marketing, product management, and sales. I have the scars from trying to drive results inside the company at every functional level as well as absorb new talent, helping them find their places, and making them productive in those companies.

My mission with this book is to be helpful to all of you who are intrigued by the possibility of joining a startup, to provide you with a framework that you can use to approach StartUpLand. In the chapters that follow, I deconstruct the startup organization and help you navigate it. And I try to let you in on a secret that not many outsiders (or even insiders) understand: *there's actually a method to the madness of startup management and organization*—a playbook that can be deconstructed and demystified for you.

Let's take the role of product management, for example. In that function, you focus on customers. You ask, *What are the needs of the customers? What are their requirements?* There's nothing scary about that. You talk to customers and try to find out what their problems are. Once you've got a sense of the customer requirements, you work with an engineering team to start designing solutions to those problems. Once that starts, you're getting into the world of product design, product development, and user experience (UX). So you focus on user testing and market planning.

Piece by piece, none of it sounds scary. As components, each of these things sounds accessible. Aggregate six or eight or ten of these components and you will understand the job. There's a box around that job. Then there are ways that job interacts with the other jobs and functions within the company.

You can get your head around that. Suddenly, it feels like there's a rhyme and reason to it.

Some people have concerns about the stability of startups or discomfort with the uncertainty involved in working for one. Startup life isn't for everyone. I get that. If nothing else, I hope the book illuminates what it's like to work at a startup so that people can say, "Oh, maybe it's not that different from working at Verizon or IBM or Target" (see the box "Is Startup Life for You?"). In short, I want to make StartUpLand more approachable and accessible for everyone. I hope to give you the tools and information you need to decide if you should turn away from the big corporate world and instead go into StartUpLand. Just like I did twenty years ago.

Once I jumped in, I never looked back. And I never did open that bottle of Dom.

Is Startup Life for You?

To help you imagine how you might fit into a startup, Erin Warren, chief marketing officer of Cartera who is profiled in chapter 4, compiled the following two lists to articulate the kinds of qualities in employees who work well in startups as compared with those who are likely to work in larger companies.

Startups

- Jazzed about doing something new

- Ability to be both strategic and execution-oriented

- Comfortable with uncertainty and flexible enough to take on a series of undefined roles and tasks

- Biased toward action

- Analytical toward optimizing your own time/resources

- An aptitude and interest in playing a broad role and evolving your career as the business morphs

A Look Inside Startup Life

To understand my attraction to startup life, it helps to understand my dad.

My dad is a Holocaust survivor. He came to the United States after World War II with nothing. He is a brilliant man and I was always struck by how his mind worked. He earned his master's degree at MIT and his PhD at Harvard. While at MIT, he developed a mathematical theorem now known as the Bussgang theorem (which to this day, I can't properly explain,

- Willing to hustle and go beyond the call of duty, even if it means sacrificing personal time

- Comfortable with rapid decision making in uncertain situations

Larger Corporations

- An interest in going deep into a particular functional area or subarea

- Strong EQ (emotional intelligence) and negotiation skills (you are dealing with a lot of people, so this really helps)

- Strong ability to advocate for your strategies and ideas in the face of opposition

- Patience (things can move slowly)

- Hesitant to put in the extra effort, particularly if it's "not my job"

- Comfortable with clear and distinct lines of responsibility, control, and communication

---

but maybe you can figure it out if you look it up on Wikipedia).[1] After a few years at a big company, he decided to start his own business.

What inspired him to start a company in this foreign country where he knew no one, spoke the language with a strong accent, and had no savings or safety net?

In reflecting on this question, I often think back to what I observed when I was a kid. Whenever my father faced standing in line—a ride at the carnival, a wait for a bank teller—rather than patiently sit back at the end of the line, he would look for a way to get around it. Not inappropriately, but always looking for an angle. He'd challenge, "Can't we design a better system? How do we push the limits a little bit?"

I'd say, "Dad, Dad—it's just the way it is. Don't embarrass us."

But I internalized that notion of pushing limits and always questioning rather than settling. It's in my DNA. When I see something that doesn't seem quite right, I push, I question, I challenge. That's how I believe you should operate in life and in business. You look for the angle to solve a problem, make it more efficient, make it repeatable, and keep iterating from there.

My dad also wanted every one of his employees to care deeply about the company. If they were to walk through the entrance and pass by the front desk and see a staple on the rug, he wanted any of them to bend down, pick up that staple, and throw it out. When you're in a big company and you walk by a staple, you think, "Oh, Cleaning will get that." My dad wanted everybody to think like an owner—to look around and see what needed to be improved, what needed to be fixed, what needed to be better. He wanted them to ask, "How do we make this place even more awesome?"

Those two attributes—pushing the limits and thinking like an owner—are critical for all startup employees. If you can program your mind to internalize those two attributes, you can fit into every startup out there.

The culture of a startup is that you're on a mission, not just doing a job. The founding team is passionate about pursuing that mission and wants their passion to translate to the entire company. A lot of startups care about "best place to work" awards and about people loving the environment. All that language is about getting people to care and think like an owner.

When you work at a startup, your efforts are clearly and directly linked to the overall success of the enterprise. When you work for a big company—say AT&T, the canonical, big, bureaucratic telephone company—you don't have this kind of impact and transparency. You don't typically have a mission to believe in so deeply. What you do each day doesn't really impact the AT&T

stock price. It's simply a job. You punch the clock. You show up at 9 a.m., you leave at 5 p.m., and instead of living to work, you work to live. In a startup, you become emotionally invested. There's a greater sense of adventure. There's a greater sense of mission and purpose. There's a sense that you're all banded together against all odds to try to achieve something no one has ever achieved before. And your work actually *matters*: every day, you're doing something that materially impacts the value and success of the company. That creates, for some people, an allure that is very special. Maybe it's adrenaline. Maybe it's a sense of community. The actual work—the tasks and day-to-day activities—may be many of the same things you might do at a big company, but it will feel very different. You're inventing. You're creating. There are no rules. No one is giving you the playbook.

That's why I love StartUpLand—because in it, nothing is "just the way it is."

Defining a "Startup"

So what *is* a startup, exactly? There's no easy answer to that question.

Purely with regard to a startup's size, I would say it's a company as small as one employee, but it can go up to maybe a thousand, or even five thousand, employees. At the stage when you are under ten people, everybody does everything. It's mayhem. Once you exceed ten employees, it gets clearer—you're doing this, I'm doing this, and someone else is doing that.

The full definition is more complicated, though, than this single metric can address. Because startups are breaking new ground, they represent giant experiments. Every initiative and action in a startup is new, and so much needs to be figured out. One hypothesis after another is being tested as the company tries to answer important questions like: *Which type of customer do we target? What precise product will we create?* and *How do we organize ourselves most effectively to make it happen?*

TABLE 1-1

Startup stages and profiles

	Jungle	Dirt road	Highway
Characteristics	Pre-product/market fit	Post-product/market fit, pre-scaling sales and marketing	Post-scaling sales and marketing
Rallying cry	"Build it!"	"Sell it!"	"Scale it!"
Number of employees	1–50	50–250	250–5,000
Profile of joiner	Risk taker, explorer	Machine and systems builder	Optimizer, enhancer

In general, I like to think of the various stages of a startup in the context of the following road-building metaphor (see table 1-1).

In the *jungle* stage, you have no idea where the paths are. There's a tangled mess all around you; you grab a machete and hack away. That's what a startup is in the very early stages. Many use the term *pre-product/market fit* to characterize this nascent stage of a startup, which means the product is not yet being embraced by customers and there is more work to do to figure out how to fit with what the particular market requires.

In the *dirt-road* stage, the path is more laid out. It's bumpy and it's winding, but there *is* a path, and the goal is to try to go down it as quickly as possible. When you're on the dirt road, you are typically post-product/market fit and you are starting to find a repeatable business model and address the early challenges of scale.

In the *highway* stage, everything is smooth. There are four lanes, and you are flying down the road at seventy or eighty miles an hour. It's "all systems go": no starts and stops, no twists and turns. It's just straight open road. This period is when you've passed the figuring-it-out stage with respect to the business model and are focused on incrementally improving all aspects of the operation. You're just executing. You're scaling more, building more, and iterating on the machine.

Is Facebook still a startup? I don't think so. Facebook went public years ago. It's a big company now—one of the most valuable companies in the world. It has exited that highway startup stage and entered full-blown big company stage. The business model is completely figured out and repeatable. Google is also no longer a startup, although both companies have cultures born from start-ups and try hard to retain elements of that culture. Airbnb, on the other hand—at the time of this writing, anyway—probably still feels raw and a bit messy on the inside. Its people are still figuring it out. From what I hear, Airbnb still feels like a startup, albeit a highway-stage startup.

Admittedly, the lines are blurry, but after ten or fifteen years of growth and maturation, most companies stop feeling like startups.

Financing is often another definitional threshold. If you're venture-backed or angel-funded, you're a startup. If you're starting a laundromat, you're not going to be venture-backed. You might be a new company, but you're not a startup in the sense described in this book.

You can also be a *bootstrapped* business, meaning the business is funded with the founder's own money or out of customer revenues generated by the business at the outset. If you have the other elements I've discussed—being highly ambitious and dynamic and fast-growing—then you can be a bootstrapped startup. But if you're bootstrapped and growing at just 5 percent a year, that's not a fast-growing startup.

In addition to being distinguished by their size, age, and financing, startups are usually high-tech, dynamic, fast-growing, and *ambitious*. Ambition is the difference. Ambition is the key.

Roles and Titles

Particular roles and titles can be a messy topic in StartUpLand, and being aware of this up front can reduce some of the confusion you're bound to encounter in your job search.

First, at a company just starting out—in the jungle—everyone needs to be comfortable doing all different things. Functional boundaries and definitions are constantly changing. As a result, early-stage companies may forgo job titles for a while. In fact, I recommend this approach. To explain why, here is an excerpt from a blog post I wrote on the subject, called "Why You Should Eliminate Titles at Startups":

> Because a startup is so fluid, roles change, responsibilities evolve, and reporting structures move around. Titles represent friction, pure and simple, and the one thing you want to reduce in a startup is friction. By avoiding titles, you avoid early employees getting fixated on their role, who they report to, and what their scope of responsibility is—all things that rapidly change in a company's first year or two.
>
> For example, one of my first bosses in the company later became a peer, and then later still reported to me. Our headcount went from 0 to 200 in two years. Our revenue grew from 0 to $60m in 3 years. We went public only two years after the company was founded. We were moving way too fast to get slowed down by titles and rigid hierarchies. Over the course of my five-year tenure, I ran a range of departments—product management, marketing, business development, professional services—all in a very dynamic environment. Around the time that we went public, we matured in such a way that we began to settle into a more stable organizational structure and, yes, had formal titles. But during those formative first few years, avoiding titles provided a more nimble organization.[2]

In other words, when you are approaching a young startup, expect loosely defined roles and some dynamism and flexibility. Titles and functional units can create rigidity: *No, no, no. I don't do that. I'm in the marketing department*, or *I'm the Director of Sales, so that's not something I would handle.* As a company grows, the distinctions can cause even more problems: *I thought I was the VP of Engineering, but now we've grown and I only manage a* third *of Engineering.*

After growing to twenty or thirty people, however, or after the first year or two, the company will probably start to need titles.

What titles exist at a startup can be a clue as to what stage it is at in its development. Even then, it's often more about the individual and about the company than it is about matching the titles in larger corporations. If I am trying to recruit you and you have ten years of relevant experience, I'm going to have to be aggressive to lure you in. I might have to give you a VP title to get you to join the company. If you're fresh out of school, I don't have to make you a VP; I can call you a director, or simply a product manager. It tends to be more individual-based than role-based. Being the VP of Product at one company may involve the exact same work that is being done by the Director of Product or a product manager or even a senior product manager in another company, but one may have more experience than the other, which allows him or her to earn a bigger title coming into a startup. The title is often a signal of what is expected of the individual when the company grows rather than what the job looks like at that moment. In other words, if you expect the employee to be an executive team member throughout the jungle, the dirt road, and the highway phases, she might be designated a VP. If you expect that a more senior person will be hired above her as the company scales, she might be designated a director.

The Organization Chart

It is helpful to know how a typical startup is organized so that you can navigate your way around the organizational chart (org chart) and move into a position that is right for you.

There are a few models. First, there's the functional work chart where each major function reports directly to the chief executive officer (CEO). Those major functions typically are Engineering, Product, Business Development, Marketing, Growth, Sales, and Finance, and each function has various subdepartments. In this book, I will cover each of these major functional areas, including the growth function, which sometimes is a direct report to the CEO and sometimes subdepartment of either Product, Marketing,

FIGURE 1-1

Typical startup organizational chart

or Engineering. I do not cover Engineering because that function, and how products get developed at startups, is so expertly covered in many other books.

Figure 1-1 represents the most straightforward functional organization.

There are a few variations of a startup org chart. In smaller companies, not every function may be filled (e.g., the sales and finance departments typically get filled in the dirt-road stage, after the product is fully developed and ready to be sold) and each of these has various subdepartments.

How the people are distributed across each function also varies over time. In the early jungle days, the focus of the organization is on building the initial product, so most of the initial employees will be in the product organization. In other cases, particularly once a company finds its product/market fit and is in the dirt road phase (after the product is fully developed and is ready to be sold), the focus of the organization tends to shift more toward adding more staff in Sales and Marketing so the company can begin to scale revenue. Sales and Finance are typically filled in the dirt-road stage.

I grabbed the organization charts of two of my portfolio companies to give you a flavor of how people can be distributed by function at different stages. In the first (figure 1-2), I show a twelve-person company that is only a few years old and just about to ship the first version of its first product. It thus has its resources heavily weighted toward Engineering and Product. In the second example (figure 1-3), I show an eighty-person company that is six years old and in the midst of scaling quickly and thus is emphasizing Sales and Marketing.

FIGURE 1-2

Twelve-person startup: weighted toward engineering and product

FIGURE 1-3

Eighty-person startup: weighted toward sales and marketing

In a growing startup, it's important to know who the founders are and what roles they play. Their titles may not match the typical pattern either in a startup or in the world of a large corporation. Misunderstanding the founder's role can result in internal political missteps. For example, a founder or cofounder may not have anyone reporting to them, but be very influential in determining product strategy. Beyond that, just know that job titles may vary wildly from one company to another.

Size Matters for Roles and Titles

Another important factor to consider is that titles are frequently relative to the size and stage of a company. The Director of Regional Sales in a corporation might have a bigger job in terms of people and budget than the VP of Sales at a startup. But in a startup—where you are able to make decisions constantly and contribute directly to innovation and company strategy and execution—you rapidly accrue far more senior decision-making experience. A VP at a startup has a lot more decision control and more complex duties than a manager at a big company, even when she has the same number of employees as the big-company manager. You may find a manager at IBM with twenty employees and a VP at a startup with three employees, but that VP, often reporting to the CEO and serving on the company's executive team, will have higher-level decisions to make day in and day out, and more strategic burdens. In a fast-growing startup, these responsibilities only accelerate.

I'll give you my own case study as an example. Right out of business school, I joined my startup, Open Market, when it had just 30 employees. I was one of the first two product managers. A year later, we had 150 employees, and I became Director of Product Management. The next year, we had 300 employees, and I became Director of Product Management and Technical Marketing. Fast-forward another year, and we had over 400 employees and I became the Vice President of Professional Services. A year after that, we had over 500 employees and I became Vice President of Marketing and Business Development, running Product Management, Product Marketing, and Business Development. At the time, I was only 29 years old!

As you can see, my responsibilities increased very quickly because the company's staff expanded from the original 30 people to over 500. If you do good work, you can grow with your startup in role and responsibility. I would have never had that opportunity at a big, slow-growth company. In a startup, your job title can change several times—not just with the shifting nature of the org chart, but because the team gets larger. Along the way, the audience gets bigger and the stakes get higher. Soon, you're making incredible and important decisions on an absurdly frequent basis.

In a startup, the sheer pace of decision making and the impact of those decisions can grow your skills so much more quickly than they would otherwise. I used to joke that I was on "startup time"—I was so dramatically challenged every day, it was like working in "dog years"—every year was the equivalent in experience of seven with an established company. My scope of responsibility increased more and more. I was always underwater and scrambling to try to keep from drowning. Meanwhile, the water level kept going up and up and up. I never felt like I was in stasis.

If you're the kind of person who finds that prospect invigorating and exciting rather than terrifying, StartUpLand might be the place for you. In fact, it may be the only place for you.

How This Book Is Organized

Since the actual work to be done in startups is such a fundamental part of how they are organized, the structure of this book reflects that organization. Chapters 2 through 7 walk you through each of the major functions of a startup, other than engineering. Those functions are product management (chapter 2), business development (chapter 3), marketing (chapter 4), growth (chapter 5), sales (chapter 6), and finance (chapter 7). You can read each chapter sequentially to get the whole picture or jump around to the functions that are most relevant and interesting to you. Chapter 8 gives you a tour of, and some tips on, the job-search process and then wraps everything up.

This is the book I wish I had read before I embarked on my own journey into StartUpLand. Enjoy!

2. **The Product Manager**

My first job after business school was as a product manager. I wasn't sure I had the right background for the job—in fact, I wasn't sure if I even knew what the right background for the job was—but I jumped into the deep end and tried to figure it out. In one of my first product meetings, I remember the vice president of engineering handing me a stack of printed bug reports as thick as a dictionary.

"What am I supposed to do with this?" I asked.

"You're supposed to tell me which bugs you want fixed before we ship the product and which ones you want us to leave in the product," he replied blithely.

"Why would we leave bugs in the product?" I asked indignantly.

"Because if we don't, it will be a cold day in hell before we ship this product," he said with a wry grin.

That was my welcome to product management.

Every technology company lives and dies by its products, and the product manager (PM) has a major impact on a company's ability to shape and produce those products. It's a demanding and complicated role. An effective PM is an entrepreneur, strategist, technical visionary, cross-functional team leader, project manager, and customer advocate all rolled into one. My knowledge of the product management function has been enhanced by the scores of students from my class who take product manager jobs at startups. This chapter tries to summarize what I've personally experienced and observed regarding the product manager's function.

As a PM, you are tied to a product and to a customer. You think every day about how to serve the needs of that customer, and how to make the product better—even in ways the customer can't themselves articulate directly. When a company is creating a new product, the PM focuses even more attention on the customer. If the company is making incremental improvements to an existing product, the PM focuses more on making the product better, easier, faster, and more robust. You might ask yourself, *How do I shape my product to best solve my customers' problems in the context of the competition, of a finite pool of engineering resources, and of the demand that the sales organization is putting on me?*

Consider Intuit's famous "Follow Me Home" program. In its early years, the company would literally send engineers to stores where they would wait for customers to purchase Intuit software off the shelves, and then ask, at the cash register, "Do you mind if I follow you home? I'm an engineer at Intuit. I wrote that software, and I'd really love to see you use it in your home environment."

These engineers would then get into their cars and follow customers home, drive into their driveways, walk into their houses, and watch them as they took the software out of the package, stuck the CD-ROM into the computer drive, and launched the app. The engineers said, "I want to see you in your actual environment. I want to put myself in your shoes."

Nowadays, the Intuit program has been modified—software isn't sold on shelves any more—but remains in place. The company does ten thousand hours of Follow Me Homes with customers each year! One Intuit executive observed that even though the approach "sounds a bit creepy . . . that process of observing the customers provides us with deep customer immersion and has helped us focus on the things customers really like and appreciate, and not burden them with things you can do but nobody cares about."

This is what PMs do. They really try to understand what it means to walk in the shoes of their customers—what their problems are, what their environments are like, what they read, who they talk to, who they listen to, what do they worry about? And then they try to extrapolate from those insights by creating representations of their target audience, called *personas*, which they can use as an anchor for product design decisions.

What's great about being a PM is that you're problem solving for a customer. You're the hub. You may not have power over every function, but you *direct* every function.

In a larger company, your responsibilities are defined precisely and narrowly. You learn some useful functional best practices if the company is well run, but you have a very limited perspective. A big-company PM doesn't necessarily get exposed to the big picture. The role is also very bureaucratic and stable, which could be an upside if you prefer that kind of situation.

At a smaller company, you have a more expansive scope, purview, and responsibilities. You get to see the direct link between what you're doing and the value you're creating for your customers.

Ultimately, startups are always on a life-or-death deadline: *You ship this product, we make the quarter, and we get financed again for another eighteen months.* When I was leading Product at Open Market, our target date to ship our flagship product was May 1996—the same time we were planning to go public. I remember the CEO cornering me in the hallway one day and pointedly declaring, "If you don't ship the product by May 1996, we can't go public. Are you going to hit the ship date?"

You don't get to have such a direct impact on success in a big company. A large company might have multiple products and an organization where a product manager is assigned to small portions of an individual product. There might be a larger strategy governing how products or parts of products all relate to each other. In that situation, you may not have any insight into how the products work together, or what that strategy might be, or how your product affects the other products, or how it's okay if you lose money *here*, but not *there*.

There could be no clearer connection between the work we were doing on the product at Open Market and its impact on the creation of equity value. Without a shipping product, the company's IPO would never have happened.

Responsibilities of the Product Manager

The product manager's area of responsibility depends on the nature of the company's product line. A lot of PMs are responsible for a complete, single product. Others oversee one of several components of a complex product (for example, being in charge of the hotel bookings platform at TripAdvisor). Still others manage a suite of products with common components or the same customers (such as PayPal's offerings for online merchants). PMs may also be responsible for strategic initiatives that cut across multiple products (for example, improving customer retention or expanding internationally).

At a high level, product managers have three main responsibilities:

- Defining the product to be built and its prioritized elements, whether a new product or an evolution of an existing product

- Negotiating and securing the resources to direct toward product development or, if the resources are already dedicated, making the business case when faced with constrained resources

- Managing product development, launch, and ongoing improvement by leading a cross-functional team, typically of your peers

Defining Products

Product definition means identifying an entrepreneurial opportunity and then confirming that it is attractive—specifically, that the proposed product or product improvement will be desirable to potential customers, technically feasible to make, and economically viable.

Once a company has decided to develop a new product, you'll lead the process of specifying the product's functionality so that Engineering can start building it.

IDENTIFYING AND EVALUATING OPPORTUNITIES. Early-stage startups are focused on pursuing the opportunities identified by their founders. In the beginning, one of those founders typically plays the role of *both* CEO and product manager (although eventually, that workload becomes overwhelming and a separate product manager is hired). In more mature companies, the core idea for a new product might come from any source—senior management, Product, Sales, Marketing, Business Development, or Engineering.

To identify and evaluate product opportunities, product teams will often engage in what entrepreneur-turned-educator Steve Blank, in his seminal book *The Four Steps to the Epiphany*, calls "customer discovery and validation."

The objective of customer discovery is to figure out if the product is worth building—whether potential customers have a need for it and if it solves their problem. Before investing in software development, a good startup will invest in upfront customer discovery and validation. So at this stage of launching a new venture, the PM's task is similar to the founder's: designing the experiments required to test the key hypotheses about how to create value for a customer.

When you're looking for product opportunities and doing your initial evaluation, your job as a PM is to collect market data; get input from the sales team; and direct customer feedback from a variety of sources, including focus groups, on-site customer interviews, customer surveys, and more. MIT's Eric von Hippel suggests seeking out what he calls "lead users"—sophisticated customers skilled at identifying needs ahead of the market.[1] Other organizations form customer advisory councils to point out trends and developments that can lead to new insights into future products. Firms also look for input from users in adjacent industries who can give an outsider's perspective that may inspire more creative solutions.

But customer data can only go so far. Great products often solve problems that customers don't even know they have. For example, no teenagers could have articulated in a focus group that they lacked the tools to connect with their friends in a playful, visual, ephemeral medium. But when Snapchat provided a platform that allowed these kinds of connections, it strongly resonated with the needs of this audience.

To get better insight as a PM, you'll often go directly into customers' environments to develop empathy for their needs and identify the pains that the product might address. Bunk1, for example, is a social platform for summer camps that helps parents and campers stay in touch. To facilitate this, the company has its product managers stay overnight at sleepover camps to get product ideas.

In a young company, you might produce little more than a few PowerPoint slides describing a product vision that articulates the core customer's needs to be addressed, the broad elements of the proposed solution, how the product will evolve over time (also known as the *product roadmap*), and a few major themes for each product release. In a more mature company, you might need more upfront documentation so you can evaluate ideas across multiple functions. You might produce a detailed description of the customer's requirements, or *market requirements document* (MRD). In an MRD, the PM will also either confirm that the new product is consistent with the company's strategy and business model or justify abandoning the product idea. In some cases, the PM might even develop the preliminary business case for a product—including pricing, competitive analysis, the go-to-market strategy (direct sales, telesales, channels, international), and sales and profit forecasts.

SPECIFYING PRODUCT REQUIREMENTS AND PRINCIPLES. The next task for a PM is to specify product requirements so that Engineering can start building the product. These requirements, which vary widely in format and formality depending on the company size and product development process, then get documented and circulated within the company so that everyone knows what the product should look like and how it should work at launch. Determining requirements is a very iterative process. As new information is gathered about customer feedback, needs, competition, and other factors, the requirements constantly need to be modified and adjusted.

Sophisticated technology companies typically establish a set of higher-level product principles that guide and constrain new product designs and influence changing requirements and feature prioritization decisions. These principles may be set by the CEO or founders, but usually the PM is involved in translating the principles into pragmatic decisions. As the PM, you might ask and have to decide on some of these questions:

- How full-featured and complex should the product be versus keeping it very simple and straightforward to implement?

- Should a new version of the software be compatible with older versions (i.e., *backward compatible*)?

- How fast does the product need to work, and when would you trade off functionality for performance?

In some organizations, these product development principles are explicitly documented at a product level or even a companywide level (like Google's "Ten Things We Know to Be True"). In others, they are communicated informally.

Based on these principles, you'll need to define product requirements in enough detail to allow Engineering to start building the product. There are two broad approaches to defining requirements:

- *Prototypes and user stories.* Many companies, particularly young ones, define product requirements by developing a working, high-fidelity prototype (in product development, *fidelity* refers to how closely a prototype corresponds to the intended product, both in visual quality and in functional representation) or even a simple *wireframe* (screen-by-screen blueprint-style representations of the high-level pages, layout, and flow that the product might incorporate). Engineers can get a much clearer sense of what to build if they can first see a prototype in action; otherwise, misinterpretations lead to guesses, which can result in design and functional discrepancies and, ultimately, to material slips in the product schedule. Prototyping helps a company get input from potential users on whether the prototype meets their needs, and it allows the designers the opportunity to learn how product components must be integrated.

As a PM, you'll also work closely with user experience (UX) professionals (described later in this chapter) to develop these prototypes, and to specify the functionality. As mentioned above, personas that represent the typical users you are targeting are frequently utilized to bring prototypes to life. The persona (sometimes called a *marketing persona* or *user persona*) is often a fictitious description of prototypical customers, encompassing their behavior (e.g., what they read, where they vacation or go out to eat), needs, and goals. Another tool, *user stories* or *scenarios*, are hypothetical descriptions of the persona completing a key task, often written to help bring the persona's needs to life for the engineering team. For example, "Melody is a working mother in her forties with zero free time. As a result, she finds it impossible to find the time to run even the most basic errands, such as picking up dry cleaning or much-needed groceries to make her children's daily school lunch."

- *Product requirements document (PRD) or product specification (spec).* A PRD or spec describes how customers will interact with a product, specifying the functionality needed to fulfill a comprehensive set of *use cases*—that is, all the different tasks customers will be able to complete. The PRD often incorporates wireframes and stories, but tends to be more detailed and formal than the prototype. The PRD has multiple audiences: Engineering, Quality Assurance,

Customer Service, Sales, Marketing, etc. Hence, it must communicate product functionality in ways that provide necessary direction to all groups. Most functions then translate the PRD into a work plan for their own group. For example, the PRD gives guidance to Engineering on what to build, but not on how to build it. A detailed PRD might specify, for example, that the login page should be secure and require email and password. Engineering can decide what specific authentication technologies to use to ensure a secure login page. Engineering typically will prepare an engineering design document that describes the architectural approach they will employ (e.g., how they will modularize the product); software languages and programming tools they will use; and the staff time required to complete the key tasks. Many engineers prefer a more detailed and specific PRD, particularly for complex products.

Whichever approach is used to communicate requirements, a common frustration for Engineering is that the direction from the PM's specification tends to be too high-level and leaves too many open questions. On the other hand, a prototype that's too detailed can elicit poor feedback during design reviews or presentations to executives. The more finished and polished something appears, the less people may think you'll be open to feedback about it, whereas lower-resolution prototypes tend to encourage more liberal, open-ended commentary and take fuller advantage of the creativity around the table.

Approaches for defining and communicating product requirements are not mutually exclusive; many companies rely on a blend of requirements documents and user stories, and the level of detail often depends on the stage of the company as well as the scope of the product or feature. Regardless of how they develop product requirements, most companies incorporate direct user feedback into the process. This feedback can take the form of customer interviews to gain reaction to paper prototypes or wireframes, and even the release of a *minimum viable product*, also known as an MVP, which is a product with just enough features to release into the hands of a customer in order to gather tangible feedback—the sole purpose of which is to test an initial hypothesis about user needs as opposed to providing a fully featured product. This approach of developing hypotheses and using an MVP to gather customer feedback and test those hypotheses before iterating further on the product is known as the Lean Startup methodology, popularized by Eric Ries in his book *The Lean Startup*. It is adhered to religiously in many startups throughout the world.

Negotiating Resources, Setting Priorities

Once the requirements for the product have been identified, they need to be prioritized, and the necessary resources required to build the product have to be negotiated and allocated. This process can be difficult to navigate, as it frequently means reconciling competing interests. For example, the CEO may want to launch a particular feature enhancement right away that's consistent with the company's strategy and competitive position, while the head of Engineering may give priority to stability and scalability of the current product, which requires shoring up the architecture and fixing bugs.

Your challenge as a PM is to satisfy all the constituents (or at least, based on your own analysis, the ones that matter) while staying true to the original product vision. One PM I know refers to this process as figuring out how to "shove ten pounds of manure into a five-pound bag."

Several techniques can be used to help set product priorities, make hard trade-offs, and fit these decisions into the constrained reality of aggressive development schedules and finite engineering resources. First, the PM can draw up an ordered list of the needed features, scoring each one in priority from high to low. The scoring process itself is a difficult and subjective one, requiring difficult trade-off decisions between major new features and small changes that might remove obstacles to sales and improve user engagement.

Second, the engineering team can provide an estimate of the level of effort required for each feature. These estimates can be as precise as a certain number of person-days of work required or more broadly categorized into size buckets of high, medium, and low. The effort required to analyze feature requests and provide estimates can cost precious time (engineering time is almost always the limiting factor) and so it should not be done lightly. Because engineering estimates are subjective, PMs need to judge whether their engineering team tends to be overly aggressive (in which case, they need to build in some additional cushion into the schedule) or overly conservative (in which case, they need to push them to be more aggressive).

Finally, there's a reconciliation process involving weighing the costs and benefits of the features required to launch the product, assessing which ones are "nice to have" versus "must have" and analyzing the return on investment (ROI) for each element of the product. The features that are "below the line" can be put in abeyance for consideration in a future release. In small companies, this reconciliation process might happen during a periodic meeting between the CEO, VP of Engineering, and PM. In larger companies, a cross-functional approval board or a more formal product council might be set up with representatives from each of the relevant functional groups. At the product council meetings, product releases are debated, negotiated, and slotted. It's like a bus departure schedule—the product council decides which features are allowed to get on a particular bus until the bus is full. You then, as PM, are responsible for driving that bus to its final destination. This can mean pushing unpopular decisions forward and being accountable for the results.

Building, Launching, and Improving Products

BUILDING. Once the requirements and priorities for the product are set, the product manager works with Engineering to make the product a reality. You'll interact regularly with the engineering team during this phase. You'll answer questions that engineers may

have about product requirements and track Engineering's progress against the plan (unless the product team includes a project
manager, as described below). You'll also serve as the "voice of the
customer" to ensure that the product being built is one that will
meet their needs.

During the building process, you'll constantly solicit customer
feedback through more customer interviews, focus groups, and
usability testing. You'll also be responsible for setting up a *beta
program*, whereby early and incomplete versions of the product
(such as an MVP or a beta version of a more complete product) are
released to a selected group of lead users who provide feedback to
the company during the building process.

The building phase is very iterative. You are constantly analyzing the feedback from the beta program and various tests, and then
collaborating with Engineering to make adjustments to features
and priorities along the way. In making adjustments, you'll evaluate
the trade-offs of decisions that could alter the product specification: *Does the appeal to customers of proposed new features warrant
potential launch delays or added costs? Conversely, would cost and time
savings justify a reduction in product functionality?* These adjustments
need to be assessed and carefully considered, as every request for an
additional feature may have a ripple effect on the schedule (sometimes known as *feature creep* or *scope creep*). Your role often involves
pushing Engineering to make changes, or, conversely, resisting
changes in order to avoid scope creep that may delay the product's
release. You will also need to communicate the changes being made
to the rest of the company so that everyone (Marketing, Customer
Support, senior management) are aligned and supportive of what is
happening and why.

LAUNCHING. A product is never finished, but at some point
you have to declare a version ready to launch and be open to the
public—known as *generally available* (GA). Some products are
launched with a significant marketing push. In the latter case,
you'll drive the product launch strategy and activities, including
conducting analyst briefings, sales and partner training, speaking

to the press, and working with Product Marketing (a subset of the Marketing function; more on this below) to develop all the promotional materials (such as website copy, advertisements, and sales brochures). Other new products, especially in companies that rely on Lean Startup methods to develop and iterate on product designs, are initially launched with little or no fanfare. Instead, the product launch is similar to the beta program described above—designed as a vehicle for feedback on the key features and business hypotheses.

In either case, it is important for you to monitor and manage early adopters' experiences during the product launch. Before launch, this requires anticipating any reliability or performance issues that might arise and developing a plan for resolving them. "Readiness" meetings allow each function to report on its progress against a checklist of launch requirements: *Have sales reps been trained? Do channel partners have collateral material describing the new product? Are the new application programming interfaces (APIs) properly documented? Have the procedures to handle escalated product use been established to route complex customer service problems to the right parties?*

IMPROVING. After a product has been launched (or sometimes shortly beforehand), you'll turn your attention to the next feature or the next new product on the roadmap. You'll also continue to be responsible for tracking the performance of previous products and features. Variances can point to problems that need to be fixed, such as a feature with lower-than-expected use due to design flaws, as well as opportunities to be pursued, like a greater-than-expected adoption of your product by a unanticipated customer segment.

Some companies have an informal look-back process to determine whether a product achieved its targeted objectives and return on investment. Others hold formal postmortems, where the cross-functional product team will debrief and discuss ways to improve the product development process.

To monitor performance, you'll rely on internal sales and usage data, including records from customer service interactions. For online products in particular, there's usually a wealth of such data. PMs should not need to depend on Engineering or the data team to access and analyze that data. You need to be your own analyst, proficient at analyzing log files using tools such as Google Analytics, Mixpanel, and Kissmetrics to pull data from disparate systems into a unified view. PMs often will develop digital dashboards to display key metrics to team members and senior management and help review the status and performance of the product after launch. One former student of mine who is a PM refers to herself as a "query and analysis monkey," because of all the time she spends running her own data queries. A strong PM watches this data like a hawk to gain information about potential future adjustments and product improvements.

After the product is released, a key task becomes adjusting priorities and revising the product roadmap—the forward-looking plan that shows when new features and new product versions will be released. You'll again negotiate with people throughout the organization to build consensus on a range of issues and make some decisions: *Should the team shift its effort toward building a new feature that is not on the product roadmap—one that customers are begging for and the sales team is demanding? What should be done about engineering's insistence that time be set aside to "refactor" code (rewrite and restructure existing software code to improve its stability)?* The PM typically lacks the authority to make these decisions unilaterally, but it is your responsibility to manage a process through which everyone can analyze trade-offs and reach agreement.

PROFILE

Yasi Baiani

Yasi Baiani, Product Manager, Sleep & Wellness, Fitbit

Having a positive impact matters to many people and contributes significantly to their happiness at their jobs. My advice is for people to really try to understand what kind of impact they want to have and at what type of company they can achieve that level of impact. Even by doing something small, you can have a large impact in a startup.

To succeed in startups, you need to be able to perform well despite all the ambiguities and unknowns. You should contribute to paving a path that doesn't exist. You also should be confident that you can deliver what you are responsible for and more with no guidance or mentoring. You also need significant tenacity and patience. Most startups are not an overnight success. You have to endure the tough days and challenges, where you are on the verge of failure, in order to achieve big success.

In order to succeed at startups and be a significant contributor, you may need to learn many new skills quickly and get out of your comfort zone. The point is that, in startups, things have to get done, and the challenge is that there are always fewer people than areas of responsibility. As a result, everyone wears multiple hats and has to do things they might have not initially signed up for.

Finally, at startups, there is no platform, no infrastructure. You have to create all those, even though many of the things you need to help put in place might have not been in your job description. This sense of building things from scratch and creating something from nothing is what makes working at startups so exciting and rewarding.

The Product Manager's Role in the Organization

As I noted above, in an early-stage startup, developing its first product, the founder and CEO often fills the role of product manager. In doing so, the founder is playing two different roles. One is product visionary and leader. The other one is resource allocator. One advantage of this arrangement is that the CEO's product vision can be communicated efficiently. The downside is that there may be less debate over the trade-offs of a given decision.

Less debate might sound like a positive thing, but tension is actually healthy in the product development process. You want to have a push-and-pull effect that results from one person advocating to be more aggressive and more visionary and taking more risk with regard to solving or tackling something big, and another person advocating to slow down in the interest of doing things right, to build something for the long-term. That tension is usually between the product leader and the engineering leader, and it's very healthy. When the founder is also the head of Product, or controls the resources, that person sometimes keeps everything harmonious and doesn't allow debate to flourish.

As the organization grows, demands on a founder's time increase to the point at which she cannot simultaneously fill the roles of CEO and product manager. It is then time to hire a product professional. Depending on this individual's past experience and the startup's policy about titles, the new product leader might be called Product Manager, Director of Product, or VP of Product. The product leader typically reports directly to the CEO but sometimes to either the VP of Marketing, Chief Technology Officer (CTO), or VP of Engineering. The reporting structure will depend on the product leader's seniority, the make-up of the executive team, and how closely the CEO wants to be involved with product management.

As the company adds new features to its first product and/or launches additional products, product leaders often assume the responsibility for multiple products, as well as for developing and overseeing the company's product management processes and for hiring and training junior PMs.

In established technology companies (i.e., highway companies), even if the product leader is not on the executive team, PMs still lead cross-functional teams. In fact, as the organization matures, the need for cross-functional leadership increases. It is more difficult to coordinate and align activities when they are distributed across a larger and more complex organization. No matter where the product organization reports (directly to the CEO or COO, Engineering, Marketing), your role as PM is deeply cross-functional. It requires you to interact with colleagues in Business Development, Sales, Marketing, Engineering, and Customer Service.

Here's what those interactions look like.

Roles of Product Team Members

Besides a PM, the cross-functional teams that create and launch successful products usually include people from Engineering, UX, Project Management, and Product Marketing. Next, I want to break down how PMs work with these roles. In very young companies (i.e., at the jungle stage), any one individual may play multiple roles, so you may also be responsible for the UX or product marketing functions. In larger companies, each of these roles is more crisply defined and tends to make up entire departments.

ENGINEERING. In well-run tech companies, there is both a close partnership and a healthy tension between Engineering and Product. Product managers design solutions, but engineers— often called *developers* in software and internet companies—actually *build* the product. To do so, they need to determine what technologies and tools they'll use, and then define the architecture for the product. In the process, engineers typically consult with the PM, who may push for alternatives. As a PM, you'll also negotiate with the VP of Engineering to ensure the product is allocated its fair share of skilled engineers. Conversely, when Engineering has budgeted too much time or manpower for a task, bloating the product's budget, you need to be able to challenge the resource-allocation decisions in a substantive way, but do so with a diplomatic approach.

Once a product is in development, effective PMs know how to hold Engineering accountable for its commitments without causing friction that goes past the healthy tension I mentioned. They also know when to push for workarounds and shortcuts that can keep Engineering on schedule without compromising product quality.

You need to have an informed response when engineers cite the *Mythical Man-Month* constraint. The Mythical Man-Month concept, originated in Frederick Brooks' classic book on software development by the same name, is that there is a limit to how much development time can be compressed by applying additional engineering resources.[2] Engineers will argue that you can't make a baby in one month by dividing the job among nine women. In some ways, they're right; it takes time for engineers who are new to a team to get familiar with a product's code and architecture and to become productive contributors. Once past that period, with strong communication and documentation and the production methods in place, more engineers can indeed do more work in less time. But this comes with the cost of additional engineering staff that may be less necessary later on.

Likewise, PMs understand the concept of *technical debt*—the consequences of hasty architectural design and coding—and how to respond when the engineering team insists it needs time to clean up its past work. Technical debt is often inevitable in early-stage companies due to platform changes, strategic pivots, and expansion of the vision. Good PMs must make trade-off decisions in every release regarding how much technical debt to incur or pay down and the downstream consequences of those decisions.

Finally, strong PMs know when and how to protect Engineering from urgent, ad hoc requests from Sales and Marketing: *Build this custom feature or we will lose the customer and miss our sales quota for the quarter!* If PMs don't protect the engineering team from the crisis of the day, the longer-term (and even shorter-term) vision and roadmap will never be realized.

UX AND UI DESIGN. The design organization typically reports to the VP of Product, but on occasion it may report to the VP of Engineering or be in a parallel organization under a *chief design officer.* Within the design organization, there will be a user interface (UI) designer, a role that typically encompasses both interaction and visual design roles. People who do interaction design (IxD)—also called user experience (UX) design—develop a framework for the natural flow of tasks that users would be able to complete. They often do this by defining some representative customer types (personas), which are based on a researched understanding of customers' behaviors and needs. These designs, which in the case of software and internet products often take the form of wireframes, are passed to visual designers, who then create the product's visual language and standards, including colors, fonts, etc. As a PM, you'll work closely with designers to test and iterate designs through rapid prototyping, usability tests, and A/B tests (also called *split testing*, where you compare one option with another side-by-side) with early users.

Interaction designers have varying levels of clout within technology companies. In many technology companies, UX strategists and directors are integrally involved in the early phases of product development and have tremendous authority in setting product priorities. In these situations, the PM role exerts less influence on product design and is more focused on process management and business decision making. In other situations, firms outsource design work or interaction design is left to product managers and/or engineers, who may have varied levels of skill in this important area. In any case, as a PM, you'll manage negotiations between Design and Engineering to ensure that the design choices reflect the appropriate trade-offs between value and time-to-market, ease-of-use, and implementation cost.

PROJECT MANAGEMENT. Project managers develop a product development schedule—usually in the form of a project flow, Gantt chart, or simple spreadsheet listing the detailed tasks and timelines. They then track progress against the schedule and ride herd on functions at risk of missing deadlines. Project managers are also typically responsible for developing and monitoring product development budgets. In creating schedules, project managers ensure that interim product releases and product development stages are sequenced sensibly, pushing back on engineering or the PM to be more or less aggressive, depending on the circumstances. Project managers also make sure that each function has been assigned the necessary manpower at the right time to complete tasks. Smaller organizations tend not to employ project managers; this responsibility shifts to the product manager or engineering manager. But larger projects will often have dedicated project managers, sometimes referred to as *product operations* or *product development operations*, who either report to Engineering or the PM.

In most organizations, the project manager reports on progress of the engineering team against plan, but does not supervise the engineers and is not held accountable for their performance. Who has ultimate responsibility for the product schedule—or, put another way, who gets fired if the ship date is missed—is a critical question that has to be determined by senior management and involves a great deal of give and take between the PM, the product's lead engineering manager, and the project manager.

PRODUCT MARKETING. Product Marketing is responsible for properly positioning the product in the market, determining how it meets the needs of customers and compares to competing alternatives. In practice, the role involves managing external parties involved in the product launch (trade press, PR agencies, etc.); training the sales force and providing them with presentations, white papers, data sheets, competitive matrix, and other collateral; organizing the firm's trade show presence; and conducting and analyzing market research. The best product marketers stay close to the customer to better understand their needs. This gives the marketers insight and influence over things like what products to build and how they should be priced. Some of these responsibilities overlap with those of Product. The distinction between these two roles varies widely by company, and in some instances the roles are combined.

Relationship to Other Functions

Besides all the product team members, the PM interacts frequently with colleagues from Sales, Business Development, and Customer Service.

SALES. As with Engineering, there is often a healthy tension between Sales and Product. Sales reps often push you to add product features that will help them close orders. In concert with Sales, you have to then decide which of these features are interesting to a single customer and which are interesting to *many* customers and therefore would be good additions to the product roadmap. Sales reps will also ask you to join in when they call on major accounts so they can leverage your product expertise and market knowledge. Working with customers in the field definitely helps you learn more about product requirements, but spending too much time catering to Sales requests can keep you from your other crucial tasks. Often, your role in working with Sales involves protecting Engineering from the interruption of the "urgent customer request" on any given day and protecting the company from one-off custom engineering versus scalable product work that is consistent with the product roadmap.

BUSINESS DEVELOPMENT. The role of Business Development (Biz Dev or BD, the focus of chapter 3) is to create and manage partnerships that advance the company's strategic agenda. For example, a firm might forge partnerships to get access to key technologies and production capacity, get assistance with customer acquisition and distribution into new channels, or guarantee the availability of valuable product complements. Many partnerships require a firm to adapt its product design to meet new requirements. For example, the mobile gaming company, Zynga (maker of FarmVille), depends on Facebook's platform for customer acquisition and has to adjust its product plans whenever Facebook introduces relevant policies or features (rules about how platform partners can contact Facebook users and such).

PMs will often join business development managers during discussions with partners to ensure that new product requirements are understood and are consistent with the product's strategy and roadmap. As with Sales, there can be a healthy tension between BD and PM where BD pushes the PM group to shift Engineering resources toward their high-priority partners while the PM tries to protect Engineering from being exposed to ever-altering priorities based on the partnership of the day. In some cases, PM will drive the BD group's priorities in the context of the product (*Who should we partner with or buy in order to meet a customer need?*) and, in other cases, BD drives the PM's priorities (*What product development do we need to achieve by when to satisfy this major partner and enable us to sign this transformative deal?*).

CUSTOMER SERVICE OR OPERATIONS. The customer service organization supports the product after it is in the hands of customers. This organization might encompass first-line customer support (to respond to customers' emails or phone calls about straightforward problems), technical support (to address more complex issues), and installation/professional services (to provide on-site training and custom development to integrate the product into the customer's environment). Portions or all of the customer service organization may be outsourced, particularly first-line support.

Early in the product development process, you'll consult with Customer Service (sometimes, optimistically, called Customer Success) to ensure that the product is designed to minimize operational burdens. Later, you'll work with Customer Service to ensure they're ready to support the product when it is released. This means product training and establishing troubleshooting procedures and guidelines for engineers in case of emergencies, like software bugs that impact customers' mission-critical activities. After the product is released, Customer Service or Operations can obtain and hand over valuable feedback to you on what customers say about the product, and this feedback can inform the priorities for the next release or suggest adjustments to help documentation or frequently asked questions (FAQs).

Depending on product requirements, you may also interact with other functions, including Legal (such as when data privacy issues are salient) or regulatory affairs. For hardware products, you'll also coordinate closely with manufacturing managers, including staff responsible for product cost estimation and procurement.

The Importance of Context

Product organizations differ greatly from company to company. So does the PM role. Usually, these differences boil down to a few things:

- Startups versus more mature companies
- Enterprise versus consumer focus
- Level of decision-making centralization
- Scale of deployments
- Development philosophy
- Business-driven versus engineering-driven

Startups versus More Mature Companies

In early-stage startups, one of the founders is often strongly product-focused and remains deeply involved in most product decisions even after product managers are brought on board. In some of these companies, decision making is centralized in that founder's hands; in others, the founder will embrace consensus decision making, and will involve all team members in important decisions. These decision-making styles pose different challenges for you as a PM. Centralized management can lead to abrupt and surprising shifts in priorities, while consensus-based management can lead to delays and decisions that are muddied by the process of compromise.

The product team usually learns from customers at a rapid rate, so these early-stage startup challenges need to be addressed by testing well-defined hypotheses and rapidly adjusting the set of features. A product manager needs to be resourceful at this stage, because it's unlikely the project manager and design professionals will be able to help. Likewise, few product development processes will be in place in an early-stage startup, so the PM must shape them.

As a startup scales, its product teams will struggle with several classic trade-offs.

- How to balance speed-to-market versus more rigorous testing and product quality

- How to sustain innovation as product roadmaps get longer and the installed base gets larger

- How much emphasis should be put on optimizing existing products versus creating new ones

- How much time should be invested in preventive maintenance of the software code base

You'll take on these and many other decisions in mid-stage companies. It can be challenging. In a rapidly growing mid-stage firm, the PM still must cope with the resource constraints of a startup on the one hand, and with the political friction and bureaucratic coordination demands that are the inevitable consequence of greater organizational scale on the other. But again, the direct impact you can have on a product and its customers is unbeatable.

Eventually, the founders hire one of two types of people to run Product. One type is what I'll call "Microsoft project monkeys"— people who document the requirements that others feed them, allocate resources, and make sure that tasks A and B and C are all achieved on the day that people said they would achieve them. The other is someone who's more strategic, someone who's going to lead Product so the head of the company can focus on other things. It's more likely that the founders will want this kind of person.

As startups grow, founders become consumed with activities that have nothing to do with the PM or the product. Fundraising takes up a big chunk of a founder's time. So does talking and communicating with investors and the board; attending indus-try conferences; recruiting and team building; and many other activities that founders get sucked into. When you see a founder spending more time on those things and less time in the weeds of the product, it's a telltale sign that as a product leader, you have the opportunity to elevate your decision-making authority.

Another signal of the breadth of product responsibility will take place in the product roadmap meeting: *Do we put feature A in or feature B? Do we put feature B in this quarter or next quarter? Who gets to say what feature C should look like exactly?* If you feel like the founders are looking over your shoulder and making those decisions, or are in the room when those decisions are being made, it means the founders are still taking a very active role. If they're not in the room at all and just ask to be debriefed later—*Let me weigh in on that one thing that I really care about; I don't care about the rest* and *No, you got that one wrong, and here's the way you should approach that*—then that means the PM has become, or is becoming, more of a leader. Having a founder remain passionate about key design or product decisions is not a bad thing, necessarily, but it does affect the scope of responsibility for the product leader.

Enterprise versus Consumer Focus

In addition to product complexity, customer type has a significant impact on key factors for success in the PM role. Enterprise customers often have diverse requirements and push vendors for custom solutions. In this context, an important task for you is to determine which features requested by early adopters can be sold to additional customers and which are idiosyncratic or customized to a single account. The challenges are very different with consumer products that have unit volumes in the hundreds of thousands or millions and where the data on customer behavior and usage is available in real time. Generally, with consumer products, you'll work to ensure the company designs a product with mass appeal, maintaining simplicity and clarity and, in many cases, incorporating elements in the product that allow it to more easily spread virally (Dropbox, for example, grows its customer base in part when users invite other people to share files through it). Consumer PMs need to be deeply familiar with the relevant distribution platforms in which they're operating, such as Facebook's Open Graph, Google's Android, Twitter, and email. With high-volume products, you'll also work with Engineering, Operations, and Customer Service to set up and solidify the infrastructure for volume surges.

Level of Centralization

When a founder is very product oriented, decision making is typically centralized in the hands of one or a few senior executives—even after the company has grown and matured. Apple was an extreme example of this under Steve Jobs, who personally decided product color palettes, among other details. Most technology companies give product managers a higher degree of autonomy in choosing product features, with senior executives weighing in only on major decisions. From a PM's perspective, a centralized structure means that getting senior executive buy-in is crucial. In such settings, once the central decision maker has set the product roadmap, there typically is a high degree of organizational alignment around product priorities, and therefore resources required to implement priorities are easy to secure.

Scale of Deployments

Some products are intrinsically more complex than others. A consumer internet startup may be able to launch many MVPs and iteratively test them consistent with the Lean Startup methodology, espousing a "launch early and often" philosophy. But other technology companies, such as Microsoft, launch more complex products—often targeting enterprise customers, whose employee training requirements reduce their tolerance for rapid product change and experimentation. Large, complex products tend to be built in large, complex organizations, and accordingly, you'll spend large amounts of time on planning and coordinating activities. Likewise, with a complex product, you're likely to be responsible for one of several product components, and thus will spend more time working with peers in Product.

Development Philosophy

Technology companies may take very different approaches to building otherwise similar products. Many technology companies rely on Agile development processes—or variations, for example, *Scrum* or *extreme programming*—through which product requirements and solutions evolve in an iterative and incremental manner through collaboration by cross-functional teams (see the box on the next page "Agile Development: Key Principles and Practices" for more background). Agile product iterations, or *sprints*, tend to be short—often one to four weeks—and each entails a full cycle of product specification, design, development, and testing. Keeping development cycles short makes it easier to debug products and reduces the amount of rework required when product requirements are revised—a frequent occurrence in fast-moving technology markets. Some companies that adhere to the Agile method deliver new releases of their product as frequently as daily or even multiples times each day.

Under Agile development, you'll often assume the role of "product owner" and be co-located with the rest of the cross-functional team, available at all times to answer developers' questions about intended product functionality. Increasingly, you'll do this in collaboration with a UX person or team, as design research is a big part of the UX purview.

Other organizations, particularly when in the product planning and prioritization stages, rely on *stage-gate* development processes—named because each stage of effort can only start once the preceding stage is completed and has successfully passed through the "gate" of a formal review. This approach is also called *waterfall* development because a graphical depiction of how stages

Agile Development:
Key Principles and Practices

The Agile development process was established in 2001 by practitioners of an emerging software development philosophy that emphasized the ability to quickly adapt to changing requirements through rapid iteration with short but complete development cycles. *Completion* encompasses design, build, and test tasks for a given product component. The philosophy's tenants were codified in a document called the Agile Manifesto, which expressed a commitment to:

- Individuals and interactions over processes and tools

- Working software over comprehensive documentation

- Customer collaboration over contract negotiation

- Responding to change over following a plan

The short cycles of Agile development mean that product teams secure feedback and adjust designs quickly: a big advantage in fast-moving technology markets. Likewise, short cycles mean that less work is completed during each cycle, making it easier to find bugs and fix them.

Agile development cycles are of a fixed duration—they are *time-boxed*, in the language of project management. They're often a few weeks. In some Agile variations, such as Scrum, all product priorities are frozen during each iteration cycle (also called a *sprint* by teams following Scrum methodologies). At a cycle's start, the team agrees on a set of tasks to be completed and prioritizes them. These tasks are often called *stories* because they entail specific actions that a user might take (like, "Open the privacy statement page after clicking on home page link"). Tasks that are left incomplete during a cycle are pushed back to the task backlog. The team never extends a time-boxed cycle in order to complete a task. At the beginning of each new cycle, the team reassesses which tasks in the backlog should receive priority for the next cycle, and which might be abandoned altogether or deferred. Keeping cycles short means that the team will not overinvest in features that are subsequently deemed to be obsolete based on feedback received during a cycle.

Each individual Agile team is cross-functional but tends to be small, typically having fewer than ten members. Team members work in close physical proximity, usually in the same room. This facilitates face-to-face communication and rapid decision making. A "client" or "product owner"—usually you, the product manager—often is co-located with the team and is available on the spot to answer questions about requirements and help make trade-offs. Most Agile teams start each day with a quick meeting in which members each briefly summarize yesterday's progress, today's priorities, and tomorrow's obstacles. This is called a *daily standup*, because people are forced to stand, which helps to limit the morning meeting to a time-boxed fifteen-minute length. PMs don't necessarily need to attend the daily standup, but often do as observers to keep close track of development progress and help resolve any issues or conflicts that arise.

Agile teams frequently release new features in small batches. At the extreme, they release new code continuously, as soon as it is finished—a technique known as Continuous Deployment. To cope with the high release volume, Agile teams tend to make heavy use of automated testing tools. To coordinate and track activity, they rely on wikis and project management tools, such as Pivotal Tracker.

Agile methods are used widely, but critics contend they are not well suited for certain types of software development, specifically:

- Unusually large projects with team members in multiple locations, causing complex coordination requirements

- Software designed for "mission critical" applications where failure is not an option (e.g., software for life-support systems)

are completed over time cascades from top left to bottom right. Stages typically include:

1. *Concept exploration*, culminating in documenting user stories and perhaps a lightweight business plan that makes the business case for the work

2. *Prototype or product specification*, the document or wireframe prototype that provides guidance on proposed product functionality, which allows engineers to begin

3. *Design work*, which in turn is followed by

4. *Product development*

5. *Internal testing*

6. An *alpha launch* with pilot customers

Work on most stages is completed largely within a single functional unit, for example, Design within stage 3 or Quality Assurance within stage 5.

Agile development may follow the same stages listed above, but in a less formal and sometimes parallel fashion that is more appropriately suited for software products that can be integrated quickly.

By contrast, waterfall planning is a phase-by-phase process more typical in hardware products like wearables or medical devices where both the risk and the cost of an error are high. With this type of product, design often must be completed before prototyping, which must be completed before development, and so on. In a waterfall process, you are likely to spend more time specifying product requirements in the formal specs. Product managers may interact frequently with developers, but they are less likely to be co-located with them, which often occurs in an Agile product development organization.

Business versus Engineering Emphasis

In some technology companies, engineering functions are culturally dominant; in others, business functions—in particular, sales, marketing, and business development—have more clout in resource allocation and priority setting. Usually, the CEO's background indicates where power lies. Business-oriented executives, like eBay's former CEO Meg Whitman, will typically build a product team that focuses on achieving business objectives—one that will prioritize products with more immediate and measurable financial impact and with more predictable development processes. Companies dominated by engineering-oriented executives, such as Google or Facebook, are more likely to build product teams that pursue elegant and ambitious technological solutions and that grant engineers more autonomy. While this approach can motivate engineers and stimulate their creativity, it also can lead to product misfires (think Google Wave) or overengineering—creating products with more functionality than the market requires.

Attributes of a Strong Product Manager

So how do you walk into a startup ready and able to talk to engineers, designers, marketing people, and sales people alike? Where does that ability come from?

Certainly, you can't learn all of that in school. And certainly you can't be a specialist in every area. The product manager role is a general management position, so PMs tend to be generalists rather than functional specialists. Although many have held both technical and business oriented jobs in the past, they come from a variety of backgrounds. Some of the best product managers are simply *great communicators.* They're clear thinkers who have strong interpersonal skills and good judgment. It's more about character and makeup and the broad skills you develop either in a professional or personal environment. Where you learn to be an effective communicator, a good writer, and a good interpersonal communicator. Where you learn to make decisions crisply and learn to handle ambiguity.

You can be a strong product manager right out of school if you have that makeup. You can also develop it over time. Sometimes great engineers become product managers because they're better communicators than they are coders. Sometimes sales engineers (this role is discussed in chapter 6) can become product managers because once they acquire customer knowledge, they want to move toward actually solving the problems their customers have rather than just hearing about them.

When good product managers hear complaints, they think, "How does that fit into the broader context and strategy?" They don't immediately think they need to solve it. Some people reflexively say, "Let me tell you about the last meeting I had, because that's the most important thing." Other people say, "I've had three meetings and two conversations and I watched something and I read something else. Now let me weave that all together into a framework with a holistic point of view that makes sense." A PM friend of mine refers to it as being able to both "systematize and empathize." That's what a product manager does.

Although the professional and academic backgrounds of PMs may vary (see "Why Liberal Arts Majors Make Great Product Managers"), most of them exhibit the following attributes:

- *The ability to influence and lead.* Product managers must be able to exert influence across the organization while holding little formal authority. Consider the challenges confronting a PM in three sequential meetings. In the first, you'll command Engineering respect to push their thinking on technical design. In the next, you'll negotiate with the head of Sales to determine which features will be prioritized and which prospective customers should be avoided due to their special requirements. Finally, you'll try to persuade the company's senior leadership to approve product strategy and allocate the resources you need. Navigating this landscape takes great listening skills, diplomacy, and an ability to marshal arguments in a succinct and compelling manner. Typically, the role requires the ability to inspire extra effort from those around them to push through difficult roadblocks.

- *Resilience and tolerance for ambiguity.* Like founders, product managers often must make difficult decisions and pursue ambitious goals with limited resources and imperfect information. Even the best PMs often make flawed decisions. Thus, you have to be willing to face the prospect of highly visible failure and do so under conditions of uncertainty, even though you lack the authority of the founders.

- *Business judgment and market knowledge.* To exercise good business judgment, it's important to have a keen sense of the market and intimate knowledge of customers' requirements. You need to be on top of the latest trends in the company's industry, attending conferences and reading relevant blogs. The best product managers have the voice of the customer in their head because they frequently speak to customers and therefore understand and empathize with their pain. Channeling the voice of the customer gives the product manager the credibility to advocate for priorities that may run counter to other managers' preferences. Likewise, your passion for your product will be readily apparent to inside and outside parties with whom you interact. Like a great entrepreneur, an effective PM can cut through the data, make sense of it, and spin a narrative that helps persuade other people to commit to her vision.

- *Strong process skills and detail orientation.* You should be able to shift your perspective smoothly between the big picture and the minutiae of low-level product decisions. It's all about maintaining focus on product vision, strategy, and ROI—but when appropriate, shifting your attention to crucial details that could have significant impact on product performance (whether by combing through bug reports or choosing the language for a value proposition statement on the home page). Whether working on strategy or tactics, a strong PM insists on getting the right data and analyzing it in a rigorous manner.

- *Fluency with technology and its implications on product design and business.* Although successful product managers have diverse educational backgrounds, all are comfortable with technology. A PM without a background in computer science or engineering must still understand the pros and cons of technology decisions and collaborate with engineers to solve technical challenges. You must be particularly proficient with your company's own technology stack—for example, reading your own product documentation and knowing the common points of integration.

- *Design/UX instincts.* Often, rather than relying on outside designers to shape the product's aesthetic, you'll instead need to leverage your own abilities. The best PMs are skilled at rapidly developing mockups and wireframes themselves with a strong design sensibility that cuts through unnecessary steps. It can take years to develop mastery in this, especially when doing it as a single part-time exercise among many other functions, but unless the startup has a UX person and/ or an interaction designer, the PM often temporarily fills this role as well as possible.

Why Liberal Arts Majors Make Great Product Managers

There is a canard rampant in StartUpLand that you need to have a computer science or engineering degree to be a great startup product manager. As a computer science major whose first job in tech was as a product manager, and as someone who has worked with hundreds of product managers, I can tell you that this line of thinking is simply bull.

The product manager role is a general management position, so product managers tend to be generalists rather than functional specialists. Some of the best product managers are simply *great communicators*. They're clear thinkers who have strong interpersonal skills and good judgment. It's more about character and makeup and the broad skills you develop either in a professional or graduate environment, where you learn to be an effective communicator, a good writer, and a good interpersonal communicator. Where you learn to make decisions crisply. Where you learn to handle ambiguity.

Guess what? Those skills are all consistent with a liberal arts education. As Fareed Zakaria puts it in his book *In Defense of a Liberal Arts Education*:

> A liberal education teaches you how to write, how to speak your mind, and how to learn—immensely valuable tools no matter your profession. Technology and globalization are actually making these skills even more valuable as routine mechanical and even computing tasks can be done by machines or workers in low-wage countries. More than just a path to a career, a liberal education is an exercise in freedom.[3]

Yes, it helps to be technically proficient. Great product managers need to know how to talk to engineering, but that's communication not coding. They need to be effective in evaluating decisions and drawing on business judgment, but that's analytical thinking not analytical programming.

I am passionate about this topic because I fear this technical bias can result in a subtle barrier for women to become entrepreneurs and venture capitalists. The prevailing wisdom is that the best entrepreneurs are former product leaders. And there is a prevailing wisdom that former entrepreneurs make the best venture capitalists. Therefore, if you believe that only former coders can become great product leaders, you are limiting your entrepreneur and venture capital funnel to a narrow pool of candidates. With 88 percent of engineers being men (an imbalance that desperately needs to be addressed, but that's outside the scope of this book), there is an inherent, perhaps unconscious gender bias at work. That's bad policy on many, many dimensions.

Beyond these qualities, I think all PMs should get some exposure to engineering in order to be able to communicate better with people who perform that function. Consider taking a few coding courses online (for example, from our portfolio company Codecademy), shadowing some engineers, attending engineering conferences (listening to the talks, reading some of the papers), or even visiting some professors of engineering and computer science to build an understanding of what they do, how they do it, and how they think about training people to code. You don't really need to learn how to code, but you do need to learn how engineers think and how software developers work— at least well enough to have context. If you don't do those things, odds are that another person applying for that job will have that skill, and he or she will stand out better to the hiring manager or founders.

I'd also recommend the online CS50 class taught by Harvard University professor David Malan. It's an introductory-level computer science class. You don't have to do homework; just watch the first three videos. Invest three hours and you'll learn a lot about computer science.

To tie all this up: the product manager's role is challenging, but PMs can have enormous impact. Product manager is a great entry-level position for anyone who wants to start a career in StartUpLand—in particular, for those who have passion for creating products, enjoy working with technology and technologists, and take pride in driving internal operating units to satisfy customer needs. Product managers at both large and small companies build skills that are useful for those who aspire to someday start their own businesses. In truth, great product managers are like mini-CEOs, marshaling the company's resources to deliver on the strategy and vision in the form of a product for the target customer.

RESOURCES

For more about the product manager's roles and skills in StartUpLand, I recommend the following:

Books

- Blank, Steve. *The Four Steps to the Epiphany: Successful Strategies for Products That Win* (2005). This book provides a terrific review of customer discovery and understanding customer needs.

- Cagan, Marty. *Inspired: How to Create Products Customers Love* (San Francisco, CA: SVGP Press, 2008). A product manager guru describes the function and its work in great detail in this seminal book.

- Ries, Eric. *The Lean Startup* (New York: Crown Business, 2011). This is the canonical guide to running experiments in startups and utilizing the Lean Startup methodology effectively.

Articles

- Ford, Paul. "What Is Code?" *Bloomberg BusinessWeek*, June 11, 2015. www.bloomberg.com/graphics/2015-paul-ford-what-is-code. Ford does a wonderful job reviewing the art of software development and the essence of programming for nontechnical readers.

Other Resources

- CS50 (course). CS50.harvard.edu. This introductory undergraduate course taught by Harvard professor David Malan provides an introduction to computer science and programming. Even watching the first one or two videos is enlightening for a nontechnical audience.

- Codecademy.com. Codecademy is an online interactive platform that offers free coding classes in twelve different programming languages. Full disclosure: my firm, Flybridge, is an investor.

3. The Business Development Manager

"I think we're screwed," I grumbled to my VP of Business Development while poking at my wilting salad at the airport restaurant.

We had just come back from a meeting with the president of a major grocery retailer, who was regarded as a thought leader in the industry. Our startup, Upromise, had this great scheme to have grocers contribute a portion of a consumer's spending to a tax-free college savings account. We believed it would drive loyalty while helping families pay for college. After politely listening to our pitch and letting us walk him through our fancy slides, the president told us he was unconvinced of the benefits of our program. He flat-out turned us down, and predicted that no other grocery retailer would join us in our mission.

My VP was an industry veteran and a strategic thinker, tenacious when it came to problem solving. "Why don't we just change the model?" he asked. "Let's see if we can get the consumer packaged goods companies, like Coca-Cola and Kraft, to fund the rewards and have the grocers just pass through the savings to the consumers."

And just like that, in that dumpy airport restaurant, we pivoted the Upromise business model, went out and struck deals with dozens of major packaged goods companies, convinced over a hundred grocery retailers to share their data with us, and ended up, in aggregate, with 15 million households as customers.

That's what business development can do for a company.

To manage the uncertainty that confronts technology startups, entrepreneurs must shape their business to fit the market—and simultaneously shape the market to fit their business. The role of Business Development is to help bring the company's strategy to life by creating and managing the partnerships that do this. Business development (biz dev, or BD) managers can have a big impact on a technology company's growth and profitability.

To be clear, when I refer to the BD function in this chapter, I am not referring to a role in Sales known as *business development representative* (BDR). That function, which is also sometimes called *inside sales* or *telesales*, is covered in chapter 6. Here, I refer to the strategic function of business development, which is more senior in nature and does not involve being assigned a sales quota.

As an effective business development executive, you're a strategist, deal maker, and brand ambassador all rolled into one. Moreover, you'll do all of these things without having direct authority over the employees who build and sell the company's products. Yet, despite this lack of authority, the "make the company" relationship is often established by the BD executive.

Responsibilities of the Business Development Manager

The core focus of a business development organization is securing a deal with a partner. Let's look at the responsibilities of a BD manager at each step of a typical deal. The steps include formulating a strategy, identifying potential partners, crafting and delivering a pitch, negotiating terms, and finally, implementing the partnership.

Formulate a Strategy

A company's strategy and business model will drive its business development priorities. Startups often lack the resources to build in-house capabilities, so they outsource activities that can be more efficiently and effectively performed by partners. Likewise, a startup's strategy determines the role it will play in its business ecosystem relative to other companies around it, which in turn determines the types of partnerships it must seek.

In broad terms, biz dev managers may structure four types of partnerships:

- *Technology/component supply.* The product team will not have the time and resources to build everything needed to deliver a full solution to a customer. Companies typically rely on other companies to supply a crucial technology or production component. A supplier may provide its product to multiple parties. (You know the camera in the back of your car that keeps you from backing up into a telephone pole? It comes from an Israeli startup called Mobileye.) Or a company might depend on a single original equipment manufacturer (OEM) that buys most or all of its products and services (e.g., E Ink–powered screens for Amazon's Kindle). Another reason to strike a technology partnership may be to extend your functionality. Salesforce.com, for example, integrates its customer relationship management (CRM) system with email automation companies so that customers can set up trigger-based campaigns to prospects that can be tracked through the entire sales funnel.

- *Operational capacity.* Firms may outsource design, manufacturing, or customer service functions to partners. For example, Dragon Innovation is a young company that provides outsourced manufacturing services for innovation hardware startups. It helped startups like MakerBot and Pebble go from early prototype to designing and building hundreds of thousands of units. Likewise, there are original design manufacturers (ODMs) who manufacture products that are designed, specified, branded, and sold to end users by a partner. For example, Taiwan's Foxconn is the largest manufacturer of smartphones, but you would never see Foxconn's brand on your phone because the company provides phones to Apple, which then sells them as iPhones under its own brand.

- *Distribution.* Many companies structure a wide variety of partnerships to extend the distribution of their product. For example, MongoDB, a database software startup, has a partners program for value-added resellers (VARs) where it works with companies that embed its software development kit (SDK) into their applications. These VARs allow MongoDB to extend its reach into certain geographies and vertical markets while its sales force can focus on larger accounts where they can offer distinctive value. MongoDB designs its partner program to provide specific technical, sales, and marketing benefits to entice VARs to sign up.

- *Platform mobilization.* Some technology companies provide platforms, which comprise infrastructure and rules that facilitate interactions between the platform's users. Platform sponsors must mobilize an ecosystem, which requires business development partnerships with different types of companies. For example, Jibo—a "social robot for the home"—has a third-party development platform that allows independent software vendors (ISVs) to build applications on top of it. These ISVs use application programming interfaces (APIs) provided by Jibo and short, boilerplate contracts that have allowed thousands of smaller partners to leverage Jibo's distribution into households. Recruiting and managing third-party partners and, in general, networks of partners that can establish credibility to a company's product are an important function for the BD team.

While mature technology companies tend to have well-established strategies, startup business models are often in flux. Founders (along with board members) typically play the lead role in formulating a startup's strategy. However, business development managers, by virtue of their training and familiarity with the plans and priorities of industry participants, are often closely involved in driving the strategy-making process and frequently team up with the founder to both craft the company's strategy and implement it through a network of partners.

Identify Potential Partners

As the BD manager, once a strategy has been formulated, you (or the startup's founder/CEO, playing the BD role) typically will assemble a list of potential partners. As a precursor, you'll likely develop a map of the industry ecosystem and analyze the strengths, weaknesses, and strategic agendas of suppliers, distributors/retailers, complement providers, and competitors. You'll regularly get out into the market, talk to investors and industry analysts, attend industry events, and visit companies to establish relationships with ecosystem participants.

In some situations, prioritizing a list of potential partners can be straightforward. For example, many e-commerce sites recruit business affiliates to drive website traffic in exchange for a share of the resulting revenue. Potential affiliates can usually be ranked easily by the size of their audience base and their relevance to e-commerce site's shoppers. In other situations, however, the process of identifying potential partners can be more challenging. For example, at DataXu, which offers a digital marketing management platform that participates in the bafflingly complex display-advertising ecosystem, the decision to partner with Google as a supplier of ad inventory was complicated by the fact that another Google division operated a demand-side platform competing with DataXu's offering. Biz dev teams need to be able to navigate such tricky *co-opetition* situations (a blend of cooperation and competition).

The desired ease of working together can have a significant impact on partner selection. For instance, on the one hand, large companies may be easier to deal with because they have better-organized biz dev units and more resources to devote to new initiatives. They also might look to create partnerships with startups as a way to sustain or boost their growth. On the other hand, large companies often have bureaucratic processes requiring the involvement of multiple organizational units. Large financial services firms, for example, are notorious for slow decision making and long trial periods, as well as for complex legal and compliance requirements that must be completed before they will partner with young companies. Moreover, after a startup has run this gauntlet, the relationship with a larger partner can be sticky, serving as a barrier to entry for the next startup. In order to fight through the many obstacles to a productive partnership, the BD team needs to be skilled at delivering a compelling pitch to accelerate the deal process with organizations of all sizes.

Craft and Deliver a Pitch

As the BD manager, you will be the one to describe the value that both sides will derive from a partnership. Ideally, these benefits will be specific and quantified. A well-prepared business development team goes to partner meetings armed with a model projecting incremental value to the partner—quantifying either increased revenue, cost savings or customer loyalty to both sides as a result of the deal.

Business development managers from well-known companies may be able to pick up the phone and get a prospective partner's attention relatively easily. Most early-stage startups lack brand recognition, however, so their BD managers must hustle to access potential partners, particularly when approaching large and well-known companies. Savvy business development executives rely on their personal and professional networks, and they also leverage the networks of their firm's senior executives, board of directors, investors, and advisers. Likewise, they are constantly nurturing new contacts by attending industry events. They also use *earned media* to their advantage. Earned media includes all impressions that are publicity derived through free editorial coverage (newspapers, TV, etc.), as well as exposure from blog posts written by the BD executive, establishing him or her as a thought leader in the ecosystem.

After securing a first meeting—which often will be with a counterpart on the potential partner's business development team—the selling process begins. A biz dev counterpart is often necessary to shepherd a proposal through the partner's organization, but this support is rarely sufficient to make a deal happen. It is crucial to find a senior champion at the prospective partner's organization in order to ensure that the deal remains a top priority. In a smaller company, the champion might be the CEO; in larger organizations, it could be a division manager, the CFO (when the deal might meaningfully impact the partner's profit and loss [P&L] profile), the CIO (for IT products), or the CMO. Gaining the support of senior line executives of the larger organization is critical, since they—unlike Business Development—control the resources and develop and secure the budget needed to approve and implement a deal.

The sales process for a BD executive is not solely external. You also need to run an internal sales effort to ensure there will be an executive champion and cross-functional support within your own organization. BD executives will often team up closely with a product manager to build internal support for the partnership, and a product manager may even be assigned to a large partner to own end-to-end success in tandem with the BD executive. In some startups, major partnership deals are subject to a formal review, complete with mini business plans and forecasts that compare the opportunity to other possible uses of scarce resources.

Negotiate Terms

When a firm decides to pursue a partnership opportunity, you'll need to assemble a cross-functional team that might include:

- Legal counsel (inside or outside) to draft the various agreements

- Product management and/or engineering staff, to ensure that the technical requirements of both parties can be met

- Finance staff, to ensure that the economics of the deal are consistent with the company's objectives and expectations

- The marketing team, to coordinate the communication and rollout of the partnership to the marketplace

- The sales team, if the partnership involves the potential sale of a new product or integrated service offering

If a partnership seems possible to both sides, your team and the partner's BD team can start negotiating the appropriate terms. This means specifying what information will be exchanged, what resources will be dedicated, and how value will be divided. When past precedent for similar partnerships provides a template for terms, the negotiation can be straightforward. For more complex or first-of-a-kind deals, however, the process of reaching agreement on terms can be time-consuming and contentious. To ensure that both sides are on the same page with more complex deals, a letter of intent (LOI), signed by both parties but usually legally non-binding, may specify—without employing "legalese"—the deal's key objectives and the main rights and responsibilities of each side. With the LOI for guidance, you can draft and negotiate a definitive agreement.

Considerable value can be captured or forfeited by the business development team during negotiations. It is critical for the team to analyze the deal's economic consequences as terms evolve and to communicate the consequences clearly to senior management.

Often, companies follow a process whereby the leader of each internal function impacted by a potential partnership must sign off on obligations.

Back when I was at Upromise, for example, no contract could be completed by biz dev without a signature from each affected department head and from the CFO, who had to validate BD's P&L impact model. Deals would get held up and it would drive BD crazy, but I would refuse to execute the contract until everyone was satisfied: Engineering, which might be signing up to develop a new feature, or the CFO, who was responsible for validating the pricing and business terms.

Implement the Partnership

After the deal is negotiated and signed, you may lead the internal implementation process, although this responsibility is sometimes handed off to another function. Depending on the type of deal, engineers and designers may need to update the product, marketers may need to craft announcements, customer service staff may need to be trained to troubleshoot new problems, and so on. As the person responsible for implementation, you'll ensure that all of the internal functions understand and follow through on their responsibilities and commit the resources necessary to successfully execute the deal.

At Upromise, our business development team was busy implementing partnerships left and right. We would sign a deal with a company to contribute money into a customer's college savings account every time the customer spent with that company. So, for example, ExxonMobil agreed to provide a discount of one cent for every gallon purchased at any one of its thousands of gas stations. Our team negotiated and signed that deal after months and months of negotiation. Then we had to figure out how to implement it. We had to connect our IT systems to ExxonMobil's IT systems to receive all the transaction data. We had to work with ExxonMobil's marketing department to promote the program.

And we had to work with its retailer network to train staff in the event that questions came up from customers. All of this was driven by our business development team.

It's common in startups to realize that it's easy to sign a deal, but hard to implement it. The priorities for both sides may change, so partnership performance against expectations needs to be monitored constantly. Even if an operations team in another function is responsible for the implementation, the business development manager's job is not over. After implementation, the biz dev team must be vigilant in ensuring that the partnership is producing the desired results for all parties and evolving the relationship appropriately. In short, the business development executive is accountable for the end-to-end success of the partnership.

How Business Development Evolves as a Startup Matures

The role of the biz dev function evolves as a startup matures. At a startup's earliest stages, it focuses on understanding the ecosystem and on building initial relationships. Sometimes those relationships are opportunistic as much as strategic—a startup might work with a partner because of a connection in the network or perhaps because they are simply willing to work with them. Mid-stage, biz dev tries to be more intentional about selecting partners and works on accelerating the pace of deal making. Initial deals will often have particular terms that require custom development work. Eventually, though, more deals will follow a standard template. At a later stage, when the startup is more mature and has a strong set of customers and partners that others want to leverage, the flow of deals starts to reverse as new startups will begin coming to you instead of the other way around.

Early-Stage

One of my mentors used to joke that, at an early-stage startup, business development was simply sales without the quota, particularly because you had no idea how to sell the product yet and so it required a lot of creativity. I discuss the evolution of the sales function in chapter 6, but many startups do simply label that first salesperson "Business Development."

Like many functions at the early stage of a startup's life, Business Development tends to be pretty flexible in how it is defined. Some founders swear by hiring a BD person at the early stages to help figure out the partner ecosystem and strike the initial deals that lay the groundwork for scaling product distribution. In searching for product/market fit and validating their hypothesis for the business model, founders may be applying crucial assumptions about the willingness of target partners to commit to the venture that need to be tested early on.

In some of those scenarios, the startup's founder/CEO—in addition to playing the role of product manager, marketer, salesperson, fundraiser, etc.—will do the initial BD work required to prove that the startup can attract key partners. Dropbox is an example of this. Shortly after launching the cloud-based file storage service, cofounder/CEO Drew Houston wanted to test his hypothesis that distribution deals with established PC security software firms would drive Dropbox's growth. Those distribution partnerships did not come easily, and so he held off hiring a biz dev executive, even as much as twenty months after the company's public launch, because he was unsure of what the business development strategy should look like.

Mid-Stage

Once they have achieved product/market fit, startups generally hire a dedicated BD executive to help accelerate growth. This executive often has either a director or VP title, and typically reports to the CEO, which helps ensure that the firm's strategy responds to ecosystem dynamics and that the CEO's priorities are reflected in the firm's deal pipeline. Alternatively, if you're a biz dev executive, you might report to the CMO/VP of Marketing, or to the Chief Revenue Officer/VP of Sales—depending on the nature of the deals and the dynamic of the leadership team. Reporting to a line executive who interacts regularly with other senior managers might help you drive cross-functional changes when implementing deals. A CEO, by contrast, may be too busy or too remote from line-management coordination issues to help you ride herd over cross-functional integration.

As your team negotiates its first partnership agreements, each deal will be custom-built. Once a few deals have been signed, patterns will start to emerge and you can achieve more standardization. As mid-stage startups increase in size and complexity and the BD function matures, they'll create a self-service option that allows smaller partners to affiliate by signing a boilerplate agreement.

Besides identifying and negotiating partnerships, BD managers in mid-stage startups often play the role of business model analysts. While mature technology companies have finance departments headed by CFOs with team members who can build detailed models, a mid-stage startup might still only have a bookkeeper or controller filling the Finance role (chapter 7 discusses the tendency for startups to hire Finance too late). In this context, the responsibility of analyzing the financial implications of new opportunities often falls to business development.

Later-Stage

As technology companies mature, smaller companies might approach them to create partnerships that offer the smaller company's technology in exchange for access to the larger one's distribution channels. As a result, a maturing company can start to get more inbound partnership requests, finding itself on the "buy" side of the business development relationship.

In mature technology companies, buy-side BD teams tend to be larger, and thus able to specialize by partner type (e.g., distribution versus technology partners), partner size (e.g., affiliates versus strategic partners), or geography. If your BD team is mature, it might also include specialists such as in-house lawyers. You then will act as a coordinator to direct the inbound requests to the right champions within other teams within your company. Hence, you need to have a deep understanding of the company's strategy, each function's priorities, and the firm's product roadmap, in addition to extensive knowledge of the firm's ecosystem.

Silicon Valley–based startup Twilio is a good example of how the BD function might evolve in a maturing company that has developed a platform that attracts others, particularly third-party developers. Twilio started out offering an SDK for building communications applications. Because the customers of the SDK were developers, the company focused on building a robust and well-documented API that developers could use to easily incorporate Twilio's functionality into their own applications. For example, the popular messaging application, WhatsApp, uses Twilio to power its calling features (WhatsApp calling).

To attract developers like WhatsApp, Twilio created a developer relations function as a subset of Business Development, serving as evangelists for the platform. The company sponsored hackathons and events and even created a small $250,000 micro-fund to provide seed money to startups using Twilio. As of late 2016, the company had over 1 million developers as users of its API in its community, up from 250,000 in 2014, and its annual developer conference, SIGNAL, attracts thousands of attendees who come to listen to best practice sessions led by other Twilio developers and employees. Strong business development, effected through expanding developer relations, drove Twilio's successful IPO in the summer of 2016 and a market capitalization of over $2 billion.

As later-stage companies grow, the BD function might expand to scout for M&A opportunities and negotiate acquisitions. Some large technology companies have a unit called Corporate Development—usually reporting to the CEO—which identifies and pursues acquisition or investment candidates. In these companies, you'll typically report to division executives (or to senior divisional marketing or sales executives) rather than to the head of Corporate Development. In other mature technology companies—especially those with fewer profit centers—the business and corporate development functions may be part of a single organizational unit. In the latter case, the biz dev team might be the source of some acquisition opportunities, but most acquisition candidates will be identified by executives in other functions or by a product team.

Key Business Development Challenges

> The most important thing you need to know going into any discussion or interaction with a big company is that you're Captain Ahab, and the big company is Moby Dick . . . When Captain Ahab went in search of the great white whale Moby Dick, he had absolutely no idea whether he would find Moby Dick, whether Moby Dick would allow himself to be found, whether Moby Dick would try to immediately capsize the ship or instead play cat and mouse, or whether Moby Dick was off mating with his giant whale girlfriend.
>
> **—MARC ANDREESSEN**

When early-stage startups negotiate deals with large corporations, they usually have to cope with some asymmetries in bargaining power. And once they're fortunate enough to gain some momentum, startups have to deal with the challenge of scaling up their own business development processes.

Powerful Partners

For startups, working with large, powerful companies can have big rewards, but securing such partnerships can prove difficult, time-consuming, and in some cases, too costly. There has to be a compelling reason for big companies to dedicate resources to working with a startup partnership, which means it can be challenging for a startup to get the big company's attention. If a startup manages to get a discussion going with a large corporation, the startup's BD staff can find itself engaged in a long series of meetings with people from different parts of the potential partner's organization. The roles and motivations of these parties are often obscure. Even when you can discern their level of support for a deal, it might often change unexpectedly. You may not even know why. It may also be unclear when and how counterparties will decide about a deal, and who has the authority to do so. And the timing of the deal can be even more opaque; while you may want to move quickly, it can take large companies month or even years to make a decision about a strategic relationship.

If it becomes obvious during negotiation that the startup is desperate for a deal with the big company, the startup's BD managers often have to guard against ceding too much ground. The startup will likely be pushed for concessions that can have long-term consequences. For example, a large company might demand an equity stake and seat on the startup's board. Such arrangements run the risk of scaring off other prospective partners in that industry. Likewise, a large company might insist on a right of first refusal to buy the startup if it receives an acquisition offer. This can chill the interest of future suitors, who would worry about entering a bidding war or being used as a stalking horse to raise the startup's exit valuation. In other cases, a big company might demand a period of exclusivity, which would carry significant—even unknown—opportunity costs.

In an interview with Harvard Business School, Dropbox's CEO Drew Houston commented on the difficulty of an early-stage founder negotiating business development deals with large corporations: "Big companies sometimes seem happy to talk to a startup. They'll bring in 12 middle managers—none of whom have any authority—to kick the tires and learn all about your technology. They'll spin your wheels for months. We got close to a deal with one of the anti-virus software providers. At the eleventh hour, they brought in an SVP [senior vice president] who announced that they were going to bury our brand in a white label deal [rebranded by the big company], contrary to everything we'd discussed prior to that point. And the SVP said, 'Oh, by the way, we'll need all this customization.'"[1]

Steve Carpenter, former CEO of Cake Financial, which provided online portfolio analysis tools for individual investors, had a similarly frustrating experience trying to license his company's data and technology to large brokerage firms: "I concluded that we were always going to be a third or fourth priority for big brokerage firms, never number one or two, especially during this [late 2008] time of turmoil in the financial system. We couldn't break into that top slot long enough get a deal done. I realized that we were too reliant on these big firms for our survival. As a startup, as soon as you're reliant on another company for success, it's going to be tough. Nobody was going to move on our time frame, so we were not in control of our own destiny."[2]

Venture capitalist Marc Andreessen counsels against founding a startup that requires a big company's support to succeed. He offers the following advice to startups for dealing with big companies:

- Be patient.

- Don't obsessively position any deal as a "do-or-die" proposition.

- Be wary of bad deals.

- Be aware that big companies often care more about other big companies' plans than about closing deals with startups.

- Hire a business development professional who knows how to handle big company executives.

- Never assume that a deal is finished "until the ink hits the paper." Once a deal is signed, the startup must be on guard against signs that the big company is simply using the partnership to learn about a new technology or product, in order to accelerate the in-house development of substitutes.[3]

However, a startup's business development dealings with big companies are not always fraught with frustration and peril. With patience and a willingness to navigate complexity, small companies can strike "make the company" deals with large companies. One of my portfolio companies was in the midst of a complex deal with a large financial services firm. I knew another founder who had partnered with the same company. I asked him what it was like to work with them. "I regret it every day," he said. "Jeff, to be honest, they put so many demands on us that they have sucked the life out of my company." Did my portfolio company walk away from the deal it was in the midst of? Actually, no. But we negotiated it even more carefully, put minimum payments and strict safeguards in place, and ended up signing and implementing a deal with the same financial services firm that has made the partnership a smashing success.

Not all deals with large companies have to be complex. Many large companies create affiliate programs with standardized terms and self-service options. Or they offer APIs that allow startups to easily leverage their platforms. In other cases, a young company can improve its bargaining position by developing a reputation as a hot startup; for example, by executing a deal with a marquee player, by securing a high valuation from elite VCs, or by recruiting a rock-star team and advisers.

Rita Garg

Rita Garg, Vice President of Business Development, Zenefits

In my role, I oversee all of the company's strategic partnerships. Our partners include companies that help comprise our all-in-one HR and benefits platform (such as health insurance carriers, 401(k) providers, and payroll providers), technology partners that help us fill internal product gaps, and strategic partners that help us drive growth and distribution.

In this capacity, I develop the company's partnership strategy in collaboration with other functional leads at the company, build out and manage a BD team, and support my team in defining, executing, and scaling successful partnership programs.

I've enjoyed working in BD in my career because it requires not only solid strategic thinking to define partnership strategy, but also deep operational know-how to ensure that a partnership will be implemented successfully and achieve the desired results. It's also a very cross-functional role, requiring close collaboration and teamwork with Product, Engineering, Marketing, Finance, Operations, Legal, and many other teams, both internally and externally. I've particularly enjoyed working in BD at late-stage, hypergrowth startups, since at this stage, partnerships can have impact at scale, amplifying organic growth, and building on a great product.

In my experience, startup life is more dynamic than working at a large, established corporation because things move faster, decisions are made more quickly, and employees can wear different hats while taking on more responsibility. However, startups often lack the formal structure and support of large corporations, so employees may have to roll up their sleeves a lot more to get things done.

At startups, to be successful you need to be flexible, entrepreneurial, creative, and willing to dive into the details to get things done, no matter your level of seniority. At a large corporation, to be successful you need to be able to effectively present your ideas more formally, and to navigate matrixed and interconnected teams across a large organization.

Scaling the Business Development Process

The time it takes to close one-of-a-kind deals can be a big burden for an early-stage startup with resource constraints, especially if its founder/CEO is still personally responsible for business development in addition to handling product management, fundraising, and other business functions. Once a startup has a template for deals of a given type, there can be big benefits to standardizing the biz dev process.

In web- and software-based startups—especially those positioned as platforms—APIs (application programming interfaces) and SDKs (software development kits) can help achieve that kind of standardization.

APIs are sets of instructions that permit one application/website to draw on the data or functionality that resides in another application/website, simplifying the task of technical integration. APIs allow the process of signing up partners to be scaled rapidly. Rather than having business development personally contact and pitch potential partners, the company can market the API to a wide range of developers in a programmatic manner. For example, when Facebook rolled out its "Like" button, it made the code available publicly so that any website—from the *New York Times* to your in-laws' blog—could leverage the Facebook user base, free of charge, thus helping drive traffic.

Firms can offer standardized business terms to partners who use their APIs, sometimes with constraints. For example, Groupon's terms of service agreement restricts API users from creating sites that are critical of Groupon. Pricing can also be simplified with APIs; companies can charge customers by the number of API calls, clicks, or other metrics. Charging more to partners who heavily rely on the API and lowering the costs for initial users makes it easier to attract smaller developers.

Many successful web-based startups have used APIs to accelerate their growth, including PayPal, Amazon, YouTube, Facebook, Yelp, and Twitter. Simply offering an API, though, is no guarantee that partners will use it. One of my partners at Flybridge, Chip Hazard, who specializes in API-based partnership strategies, has the following recommendations for early-stage startups trying to build an API user base:

- *Rapid time to value.* Developers, like everyone else, are stretched for time, so the product needs to show value fast. Traditionally, this means being able to get up and running in less than thirty minutes—if not sooner.

- *Free to start.* Many companies begin with a fully functional, high-value, free product that allows experimentation. Asking for payment before establishing value can be an obstacle to developer adoption.

- *Superior documentation and support.* Develop easy-to-use and clear documentation to address any support needs quickly and thoroughly. Setting up robust support forums and enlisting the entire company in participating in them will provide high-value assistance to the customers. Ideally, provide analytic tools that show the value that users derive from the API.

- *Facilitate word of mouth.* Get your customers to speak on your behalf, either live or via their own blogs or social media outlets such as Twitter. Share presentations and case studies via SlideShare. Contribute positive reviews and comments to developer content sites like Hacker News and Stack Overflow. Slick marketing doesn't work because developers are smart and cynical, so build credibility by providing authentic value.[4]

Not all mature business development functions are API-based. Many companies are simply focused on signing and implementing more distribution deals, channel relationships or platform partnerships. No matter what the focus, as a startup matures, there is a growing emphasis on standardization and profitability. Often, this requires the early business development deals to be renegotiated. The early-stage startup might have been more desperate or naive about what the partnership should look like as compared to a few years later when the business is more experienced and mature.

Attributes of a Strong Business Development Manager

The professional backgrounds for BD people can vary widely, but most successful BD managers in startups have a few key attributes:

- *Networking skills.* When looking for partners for a young startup, a broad professional network gives you access and credibility. The ability to develop new contacts is also vital, and you should be comfortable representing your company with senior counterparts. These networking and relationship-building abilities can be honed through sales experience, but in firms where automated, self-service deals are the norm, a sales mindset may be less well suited for business development.

- *Market knowledge and strategic perspective.* To identify promising partnerships, it's important to have a deep understanding of the strengths, vulnerabilities, and strategic agendas of all the participants. You also should be able to project how the whole ecosystem might evolve. Strategic planning frameworks and raw intellectual horsepower can substitute to some extent for domain expertise, but it's hard to replicate the knowledge and social capital that you can build up over years of working in a given industry.

- *Negotiation skills.* BD managers negotiate constantly—not only with counterparties, but with executives in other functions within their own company. Great negotiators have diverse styles, but they all have a knack for devising creative, win-win solutions, building trust, keeping their emotions under control during stressful negotiations, and knowing when to press advantage, when to bluff, and when to walk away from the table. One of my former students, who is a biz dev executive, likes to say that the role is more like that of a politician than that of a salesperson. You can sharpen many of these abilities through training and experience, but some come from innate intelligence and psychological predisposition. Also, deal making has many technical aspects, so being a BD executive means having a good understanding of common contract provisions and when they might be used most effectively (for example, rights of refusal, nondisclosure agreements, change of control provisions, exclusivity arrangements, and so on).

- *Analytical skills.* Since many partnerships are one-of-a-kind, you should be comfortable with business model analysis and economic/financial modeling. In this effort, you will collaborate with the finance department, but sometimes a startup's finance department might be weak or nonexistent and you'll have the burden of the analysis on your shoulders.

- *Entrepreneur's mindset.* Just like company founders, you'll frequently act as the public face of the company, pitching the company to outsiders. You also must make difficult decisions and pursue ambitious goals with limited resources and imperfect information. (This is the ever-present joy of StartUpLand!) Even the best BD managers often make flawed decisions. You have to be willing to face the prospect of highly visible failure, and to do so under conditions of great uncertainty.

- *Product knowledge.* As a business development professional, you'll need to have a strong understanding of the company's product and services, particularly its value proposition in comparison with competitive products, in order to prioritize potential partnerships and to pitch them effectively. Product and technical expertise is particularly valuable when it comes to getting involved with the development of APIs. You don't necessarily need to be a programmer, but you should at least be familiar with your own product and how customers use it. Finally, for deals requiring new features or design modifications, product knowledge is useful when overseeing implementation work that Engineering is doing. Experience in product management can provide a good background for undertaking the BD job, but a basic understanding of the attributes of a good product and how to generate and validate product requirements can also be sufficient.

The BD role in a startup is a challenging one that can have enormous impact (of course, this is true of most positions in an early-stage company). Business development is a great entry point into StartUpLand for talented young professionals looking for careers in technology companies—in particular, for those who prefer a role more outward-facing than that of, say, product manager, or a role that involves less structure and more creativity than entry-level positions in Marketing and Sales.

RESOURCES

Good resources about business development in StartUpLand include:

Books

- Brenner, Bernie. *The Sumo Advantage* (2014). By the cofounder of TrueCar. A sweeping, strategic review of how to engage big companies in win-win partnerships.

- Taub, Alexander, and Ellen DaSilva. *Pitching and Closing* (New York: McGraw-Hill Education, 2014). Taub is CEO/ founder of SocialRank and DaSilva a former executive at

Twitter. This book gives a tactical guide to the business development role and how a business development executive can operate effectively.

Other Resources

- *Platforms and Networks: Insights and Resources for Tech Entrepreneurs* (website). http://platformsandnetworks .blogspot.com/p/business-development.html. HBS Professor Tom Eisenmann has a great, curated directory of the best business development blog posts on this site.

4. Marketing

When I was head of Marketing at one of my startups, our sales director in Australia came to our annual sales meeting bearing a gift for me: a boomerang. He said it was because I always came back to him with answers to his questions when he was in the field chasing sales opportunities. I keep that boomerang in my office to this day and still think about how much field salespeople appreciate it when the marketing team gets back to them in a timely, responsive fashion. For a marketing executive, being customer focused means paying attention to your internal customers as well as your external ones.

When entrepreneurs discuss with me the reasons they need to raise money for their startups, the focus is typically placed first on building the product and then selling it. The two most expensive functions at a startup are the product team and the sales team. Marketing profoundly affects them both: on one side, it heavily influences product design; on the other, it focuses and supports Sales. So the marketing function is like the productivity engine of the startup. When a startup has a great marketing function, the product and sales teams both look amazingly productive, and nobody knows why. Everybody typically credits the head of Sales and the head of Product, but behind the scenes, it's Marketing that makes them look good.

Marketing, in other words, is the unsung hero of the startup.

Context and Organizational Evolution

Strangely, startups often hire marketing people too late. First they hire the team required to build the product—product managers or engineers. Then they hire one or two salespeople to sell the product. Remember the organization chart for my twelve-person startup in chapter 1 (figure 1-2)? There are zero marketing people. It's a common mistake.

Typically, the first marketing person might get hired as employee number twenty or thirty, often after a startup hits a snag. Perhaps the sales force has become unproductive and is idling. So the startup scrambles to get a marketing function installed quickly to help. By then, though, it's often too late. When a startup misses its sales numbers, the salespeople get blamed. But the problem, typically, is *not* that the salespeople are incompetent; it's that the startup lacks marketers who can generate leads and acquisitions for those salespeople. As a result, Sales is either getting bad leads or no leads at all. They're lacking the good, competitive weapons that skilled marketers can provide, so they're struggling to win.

That's when the company needs Marketing. It needs Marketing to provide support for Sales.

My personal preference is for the marketing function to be in place before the initial product launch, even if the entire function is one person who serves as a generalist. Before a startup launches a product, Marketing is often the function that teams with product management to manage the beta (early customer) or pilot program. At an enterprise company, Marketing helps recruit beta customers, gets them familiar with the product, and holds their hands through the beta process, making sure they have a positive experience with the product and are willing to serve as a reference to others. Meanwhile, Marketing listens carefully to the beta customers, using their feedback to help shape the marketing message and clarify the value proposition. While the product manager may be formally tasked with prioritizing what goes into the product, Marketing often helps arrive at those decisions. Once the product is near shipping, Marketing should be there to help customers get up to speed, talk to those early adopters, write up their use of the product as a case study for others to learn from, secure them as references, and encourage them to be spokespeople with the press. That way, when the product is launched, the startup has all the marketing tools it needs at its disposal to establish credibility and get the word out.

Because it is so easy to equate Sales with revenue, startups tend to overinvest in Sales and underinvest in Marketing. Let's say that every additional sales rep at a hypothetical startup adds another $1 million in revenue. The math is easy; if the startup wants to grow $5 million more in revenue, it should just hire five more sales-people. As it turns out, however, one or two marketers who can help create demand and pull can take a startup *from $1 million per sales rep to $1.5 million per sales rep*—because marketers help the sales team become more efficient and more productive.

That's the magic of hiring a good marketing team.

Structure of the Marketing Function over Time

In an early-stage company, the first one or two marketers have to be generalists and do everything. In a company with very little budget and very little money, you've got to be scrappy and creative, and the staff may be where most of the investment is.

As the company gets into a little bit more of a growth mode and more resources are dedicated to marketing, the group begins to specialize. That's where the context changes. As a company grows to the point where it establishes a marketing budget, it allocates dollars to use to run marketing programs; attend events; and create marketing programs like advertising, webinars, lunch-and-learns, and speakers who go to cities to speak to customers, trade shows, and user conferences. Sometimes companies will spend dollars to develop email- or direct-mail programs they want to pump out. Those are all variable costs in the form of marketing program dol-lars that can be ramped up or down quickly. A startup might double its marketing investment in program dollars without increasing marketing staff.

Note that above is the first time I've used the word *advertising*, a word that in the old days was synonymous with marketing. Not anymore.

A friend at business school, who sat next to me for our entire first year, liked to joke that the answer to solve every business case was, in the end: "Increase your advertising budget." Want to increase sales? *Do more advertising. Buy more TV time, buy more radio time, buy more newspaper time.* It's really simple.

Nowadays, certainly, that has changed. There's a general view now that old-school advertising doesn't work in StartUpLand. Ramping up your marketing requires more creativity. Maybe that's a person who does content marketing. Maybe it's a growth hacker. Maybe it's an evangelist. Maybe it's a community manager.

In early-stage companies, someone—a generalist—does *all* of this. Over time, people become more specialized. The people who are great at MarCom (marketing communications) or corporate marketing are very different than the people who are great at lead generation, for example. Typically, each role is handled by a different kind of person because the marketing function has so many subdisciplines.

At Open Market, when I ran marketing, the peak size of my department represented roughly 10 percent of the entire employee base. At that scale, I had VPs for each of the different marketing functions, and directors and managers underneath them and all that. That department was built over five or six years, very rapidly— from zero to sixty-five people. In a smaller company, such as my eighty-person portfolio company whose organization chart appears in chapter 1 (figure 1-3), those departments and functions might be covered by a much smaller team, as few as five or ten people. A smaller department just requires everyone to wear several different hats, which is fundamental to how things work in StartUpLand.

In their early days, many startups stick the first few marketing professionals under the head of Sales or the head of Product because they may not be senior enough to warrant reporting directly to the CEO. And it may be too early to hire a senior executive to lead Marketing as compared to a few, more junior doers. Over time, most of the people who serve in these marketing functions report to a head of Marketing, who might be called Director of Marketing or Vice President of Marketing or even Chief Marketing Officer, depending on their seniority and how large the marketing organization is. These functions include product marketing, MarCom, and demand generation. Although MarCom may report to the VP of Marketing, this role is often joined at the hip with the CEO, as the CEO handles announcements, events, and speaking engagements.

A startup might also have a customer acquisitions role, with social media marketing and email marketing people reporting to that person, although social media can also report to MarCom.

If the company sells its product through a channel, or if it has partners and drives marketing activities through them, then channel or partner marketing functions might also report to the head of Marketing.

Functions and Responsibilities

So what's involved in the marketing profession in the context of StartUpLand? Startup marketing is all about a dynamic blend of creativity, analytics, and science. The way these elements are applied is always changing. There has been a lot of evolution and innovation in recent years around the role of marketing, which together have made the role even more compelling and strategic.

In the classic world of marketing, there exists what is called the *marketing funnel*. At the top of the funnel, you generate awareness and interest in your product. In the middle of the funnel, you educate prospective customers and establish preference, getting them to engage with you to learn more. At the bottom of the funnel, you try to convert prospects into actual customers. In StartUpLand, there have been a number of innovations in how the marketing funnel is implemented, all of which affect the role and responsibilities of the marketer in the organization.

Top of the Funnel: The New World of Content, Inbound, and Social Marketing

A primary job of Marketing is to feed qualified leads to Sales, and the science of lead generation has gotten much more sophisticated in recent years. Content marketing, inbound marketing, and social media marketing now have enormous impact. With their nascent brands and immature distribution channels, startups focus on breaking through the clutter by generating high-quality, engaging content that leads to discovery and awareness among prospective buyers. Those prospects can then learn about the startup and its offering without being bombarded by push marketing, which can be interruptive and annoying. Many people who have never responded to a telemarketer or a direct mail piece will respond to a piece of informative content they read on the web or a piece of content they saw on social media streams. Further, many people research a product online and purchase it as a result of content they discover. Because of this, content marketing and inbound marketing have exploded and marketing departments at startups are looking for greater expertise in those areas.

In the context of this new world of content-based marketing, startups are looking for marketers with a different set of skills than many big companies. The ideal startup marketer is a good writer, effective at crafting emails that yield engagement; competent at generating slide presentations that inspire easy sharing; skilled at producing webinars and videos; and, all in all, able to drive awareness and interest through a deep understanding of the customer.

In today's social media–driven marketing environment, marketers are not just skilled at writing long-form material (white papers, website copy, product data sheets) but also producing creative short-form content that fits into the typical social channels. That means creating a funny GIF or thought-provoking 140-character tweet that can be shared widely. In recent years, Snapchat and Instagram have become important marketing channels for some startups. Thus, being facile with creating Snapchat Stories or Instagram Stories and memes may be valuable as well. Whatever it takes to get views, likes, and shares falls to the marketer.

Bottom of the Funnel: The New World of Analytics, Conversion, and Freemium

While those developments are happening at the top of the marketing funnel, a rigorous world of analytics, engagement, and conversion science happens in the middle and end of the funnel.

There used to be an old saying in marketing, attributed to nineteenth-century retail magnate John Wanamaker: "Half the money I spend on advertising is wasted; the trouble is, I don't know which half." Well, in the era of "big data meets marketing," that problem is no longer prevalent. Marketing has become a science. Analytical tools and online frameworks allow the marketer to have much more transparency and visibility into every individual person who makes every individual click and view on some piece of advertising. Research firm Gartner famously predicted a few years ago that the Chief Marketing Officer would spend more on information technology than the Chief Information Officer by 2017.[1] Analytics tools like Google Analytics, Adobe Omniture, Domo, Kissmetrics, InsightSquared, and Mixpanel are becoming as common in marketing departments as desktops and smartphones. And nowhere have these marketing innovations been more prominent and widely adopted than in StartUpLand.

Another marketing innovation popular in StartUpLand is the freemium business model. In this model, a company uses the product itself as the marketing tool and offers a free version. Customers are asked to pay for a premium version of the product only once they have used the product, understood and appreciated its value, and had gotten addicted to it. Dropbox is a great example of this. People use this super-simple file-sharing and synchronization product, fall in love with it, and start storing their files, pictures, and videos in it. It's easy and it's free. Over time, the user hits a storage threshold and is offered the option to pay for more storage space. And if users share Dropbox with a certain number of friends, they get even more storage.

Think about that.

The free storage and the high-quality product have an effect on Dropbox's marketing: the combination draws people in, builds the customer base, and then drives conversions to the paid model and/or customer acquisition among users' friends when users run out of free storage. Employing the freemium model and utilizing this kind of referral rewards technique have been a very popular marketing tactic in both consumer and enterprise startup businesses. Today's marketer thus needs to be facile deeper in the funnel, understanding the precise levers that lead to customer and sales conversion.

The role of the marketing department throughout the funnel varies for a company targeting consumers (business-to-consumer, or B2C) as compared to one targeting businesses (business-to-business, or B2B). B2C companies typically do not have a sales force—or if they do, it's a sales force focused on selling to advertisers rather than end users. In this case, Marketing's role is less about driving qualified leads to sales and more about driving acquisition, retention, and the desired behavior (e.g., in the case of Instagram, posting more photos). That said, some B2C companies go to market like a traditional B2B company and vice versa, so these distinctions have points of overlap. For example, my portfolio company Open English is an online school for English language learning. The conversion process looks more like a B2B conversion funnel—marketing generates leads and directs those leads to a telephone-based sales force that tries to convert the prospects into paying customers. The point is that there are many variations on the theme of marketing and how it prioritizes its efforts up and down the funnel.

Baseline Skills for Marketers in StartUpLand

Beyond these more innovative areas, there are a few things every marketer should have in her pocket as a baseline of skills, in addition to the classic basics of good communication and writing skills.

A/B Testing

A/B testing is the testing of two different designs or task flows, or simply two versions of the same page, and exposing them in equal weighting to a section of customers to see how they react. For example, say an e-commerce company wants to know the difference in outcomes between putting the "Buy" button at the top of the page versus the bottom of the page. An A/B test allows you to see what the conversion rate looks like in each scenario as compared to the rate of shopping cart abandonment. You keep testing whether the button should be placed in different spots, shown in different colors or in different sizes, and how it performs with different calls to action (e.g., "Buy Now" or just "Buy"). And you keep testing and testing all these different permutations, choose the best outcome between A and B, and then you test the other parameters, holding all other variables constant. It's like a big science experiment applied to software products.

The marketing software company Hubspot is an enthusiastic A/B tester. In one test, it compared two different ways to get customers to sign up for a free white paper: in one case (scenario A), the signup form was embedded in a blog post and in the other case (scenario B), the signup form was accessible through a separate link off the blog post. The embedded signup performed 71 percent better. Guess which signup model Hubspot used going forward?

Unit Economics

Next, an understanding of unit economics is critical in the marketing function. When I say *unit economics*, I mean comparing the customer acquisition costs (CAC) with the lifetime value of the customer (LTV).

Marketing people at startups are the gurus of unit economics because they're always measuring CAC versus LTV and using this data to inform the company about how it should invest in Sales and Marketing. A lot has been written by me and others about the proper way to calculate CAC and LTV. I won't repeat it here but it's available on my blog, *Seeing Both Sides* (seeingbothsides.com). Suffice to say, the marketing function needs to be smarter than everyone—even Finance—at calculating these figures and deriving from them the appropriate implications.

Cohort Analysis

Another important tool in figuring out unit economics is conducting *cohort analysis*—organizing customer behavior data into related groups and analyzing each group, or cohort, to determine trends over time. Examples of common cohort analysis include tracking customers who began using a service at a given point in time and seeing how they behave month over month, or how the customers who were acquired via a particular source perform month over month. Suppose, for example, it costs you ten cents in advertising and marketing costs on Facebook to drive an installation of the popular augmented reality gaming application, Pokemon Go. When you do your cohort analysis on the Facebook-acquired users, you observe that they never actually use the product—they just install it and abandon it—and thus are worthless to you. Then, suppose you launch another customer acquisition initiative on Snapchat where each user costs you twenty cents to acquire, but when you do your analysis of this cohort of users and how they behave over time, you observe that these users play Pokemon Go incessantly—twenty times a day, every day, month after month after month. Thus, your cohort analysis shows that the Snapchat-driven acquisitions are far more valuable than the Facebook-driven acquisitions.

Cohort analysis lets you truly understand your customer acquisition cost and your lifetime value math in the context of particular channels and post-acquisition performance.

Demand Waterfall

A valuable framework to understand the entire marketing funnel in an analytical fashion is the *demand waterfall*, also referred to as the demand generation waterfall. Each stage of the customer journey is mapped out and a percentage conversion is assigned to each in order to provide a mathematical equation that helps predict outcomes. For example, as shown in figure 4-1, a company might indicate that a

FIGURE 4-1

Demand waterfall

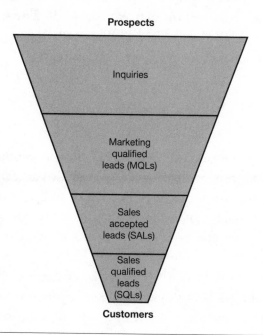

certain number of inquiries from prospective customers results in a marketing qualified lead, or MQL (e.g., when a prospect from a relevant target organization provides an email address or downloads a white paper). MQLs might be defined by the prospect's profile (title, company) or the actions they take. An MQL is handed over to the sales team and then goes through a further qualification process to be accepted by Sales as a sales accepted lead (SAL). After the sales team has worked a lead long enough to determine it has a high potential of closing, it becomes a sales qualified lead (SQL).

Some percent of MQLs become SALs, some percent of SALs become SQLs, and some percent of SQLs become customers. Put these pieces together and you have the demand waterfall—a mathematical formula that tells you what your conversion percentage looks like at each stage of the process. This is a very useful tool for marketers and sales teams alike because it helps define the marketing budget. If the company is aiming to achieve a certain number of sales, it simply does the math backward up the funnel to determine how many MQLs are required to generate the necessary SALs, SQLs, and, ultimately, sales. The marketing team should know how much it costs them to generate leads and thus can predict the number of leads it will generate based on the market budget it is allocated. Figuring out what the demand waterfall looks like and, importantly, how to improve it and make it more efficient is a critical role of the marketer.

Network Effects

One key element in a startup's strategy is the application of network effects and startup marketers need to be skilled at identifying and amplifying this strategy. Network effects can be present in startups in obvious and nonobvious ways, and many startups focus on creating network effects in their business to achieve competitive advantage.

Network effects exist when the value of the network increases with the number of people who participate in the network. LinkedIn is a great example. If only one person is on LinkedIn, it's pretty useless; if every single one of your professional colleagues is on LinkedIn, it's pretty valuable. And if the entire world is on LinkedIn, it's even *more* valuable.

Network effects are such a powerful and important element of startup business models that at my firm, Flybridge Capital, when we score each startup, we evaluate it based on the strength of its network effects. The reason venture capitalists are so focused on network effects in startups is that they can result in a "winner-take-all" market dynamic where the largest networks become so much more valuable than their competition that there is no reason to join one of the smaller networks. This competitive advantage continues indefinitely, allowing the company to outperform its competitors for many, many years.

Airbnb is a nice example of a business with strong network effects and a winner-take-all dynamic. Serving as an online marketplace to secure short-term home or apartment rentals, Airbnb is a two-sided market that becomes more and more valuable to consumers as there are more listings (more options to stay in more cities) to choose from, as well as to the property owners as there are more and more consumers to rent to. Thus, the company has catapulted from its founding in 2008 to serving over 150 million guests in sixty-five thousand cities and being valued at $30 billion—more than the valuation of storied brands like Hilton and Hyatt combined.

Consumer-based networks like Airbnb, Facebook, LinkedIn, and Snapchat have educated people on social media–based properties that have strong network effects, but there are also very strong network effects in less obvious, more technical businesses. One of our portfolio companies, ZestFinance, uses machine learning to underwrite loans for consumers, specifically subprime or near-prime consumers. And the reason that underwriting algorithms have very powerful network effects—and this is true for most machine learning–based business models—is that the models get smarter and smarter with more data. The more people there are who apply for loans, the more the model is trained; the more people who default or pay back loans, the more the model is trained in correlation. The model is continuously updated, analyzed, and improved as it gets exposed to more and more data. After you get enough data, you have a much, much more valuable model, trained on far more data than when the business first started and made its first loan.

You can see these data-driven network effects in a lot of enterprise businesses and data-intensive applications. Google Search contains strong data-driven network effects because the more searches people perform and the more time Google watches people click on search results, the better the outcome and the better Google can succeed in having the next search outcome be even more accurate. In fact, it's no coincidence that the former VP of Engineering at Google is the founder of ZestFinance and has a PhD in machine learning from Princeton. Marketers don't need to be PhDs in machine learning, but they do need to understand network effects and their impact on marketing strategy.

Goal Setting in Marketing

Logistically, here's how Marketing's goals get set. When the annual plan gets developed, it gets broken up by quarters. The CEO hands out goals and then turns to the head of Sales and says, "What's our revenue number going to be?" The head of Sales then picks a number, and the CEO proceeds to negotiate, pushing it higher or lower, depending on the circumstance (most typically higher!). The head of Sales then turns to Marketing and says, "If we're going to sign up $5 million in revenue, then based on our typical conversion rate from past years, that means you need to generate two thousand leads. Can you generate two thousand leads?"

So Marketing says, "If I'm going to generate two thousand leads, I need the following budget because I have a certain cost per lead, and I need the following staff."

The two sides negotiate back and forth, and then the CFO gets involved and helps balance it all out.

Then they turn to Product, because Sales and Marketing both say, "We can't generate these leads and we can't make these sales targets unless the product team delivers these new features."

Product comes back with, "Okay. Based on what I'm hearing from Engineering, we need this large a development organization to build those features, and this is when I'll be able to ship that product with those features."

They go round and round and back and forth. When the annual plan is done, Marketing signs up for its target number.

Now comes the dangerous part. If the company misses its numbers, the first person to typically get fired is the head of Sales. In this case, the Sales VP would say, "I'm behind in achieving $5 million because there weren't enough high-quality leads or the product was late and the features weren't what they said they would be." But if the Sales head can't hit $5 million, the company needs to find someone who can.

The second person to get fired is the head of Engineering, because (typically) either the product missed its ship date or the features aren't what they said they were going to be.

All the while, the head of Marketing gets to hide behind Sales and Engineering. The head of Marketing is typically the last person to get fired.

I said before that Marketing is the unsung hero. It can also be the unsung villain.

PROFILE

Joe Chernov

Joe Chernov, Vice President of Marketing, InsightSquared

> Over my last four roles, I've gone from leading a marketing function (content marketing) through a growth-stage startup's IPO, to leading all of Marketing at an early-stage startup, back to leading a functional group through an IPO, and again back to owning all of Marketing at a startup. I've worked in thousand-person companies, hundred-person companies and ten-person companies. I've never worked for a large multinational.

My specific responsibilities in both VP of Marketing roles are similar, as were my specific responsibilities as the content marketing leader. [But] as you might expect, there's more pressure to prove business results as VP of Marketing. When you lead a subgroup within Marketing, there's pressure to continually improve the quality your team's output—and while that includes ratcheting up key performance indications [KPIs], it also applies to the work itself. But because one group's KPIs converge with others' to produce business outcomes (for example, if the blog team succeeds at driving traffic and the demand generation team succeeds at converting those readers into sales leads, then the team overall has a chance to meet its revenue goals. But in this scenario, neither the blog leader nor the demand generation leader is alone accountable to top-line growth)—there's some "safety" in being the stop before the buck stops. As the VP of Marketing, you are responsible for business outcomes, not marketing activities or even directional KPIs. This absolute accountability shapes your focus—if generating pipeline is the challenge, then you need to marshal all your resources to sourcing quality leads; if deal size is compressing, then your responsibilities flip to late-stage sales support. "Prioritization whiplash" is an occupational hazard for the head of marketing.

What appeals to me about startups is being part of the "becoming" of something. *Becoming* is always more interesting than *became*. There's a personal reward to be found in helping define, shape, and grow something. If seeing your thumbprint on a company matters to you, then startups may be an attractive career. I didn't go into startups thinking about this aspect of the reward, nor did I realize that long after an exit, there emerges an incredibly deep connection with the people who left their thumbprint alongside yours— but these deeply personal experiences are very much part of the startup allure.

It's a bias toward action coupled with a willingness and courage to fail. The attractiveness of each of these qualities is inversely proportional to company size.

If companies were roadways, startups are a network of red lights and green lights: *Do this; stop doing that. We're launching this; we're sunsetting that.* Because at a startup, there's always much more to do than there are people to do it, decision making is pushed closer to the edge. Necessity is the mother of invention. *Failing forward*—failing, but learning something in the process—is considered healthy in startups. Conversely, larger companies are ruled by yellow lights. A great idea can be derailed because, at the margins, it crosses into another group's territory or requires a different function's resources. Protectionist behavior tends to increase as a company grows and failure is typically less tolerated in larger companies, yet readily encouraged in smaller companies. For example, I had a startup CEO who correctly observed that the marketing team was so averse to failure that it was suppressing our willingness to experiment. To combat this behavior, he introduced an annual "Biggest Flop" award to the marketer whose campaign failed, but where the organization learned something as a result.

Marketing Roles

Corporate Marketing

Corporate marketing, or MarCom (marketing communications), is focused on brand public relations (PR) and communication. In this role, you're the one organizing events and meetups, writing the press releases, designing (or facilitating the design of) the website, and setting up speaking engagements for the founders. You're designing the logo and the design palette for branding purposes. Your tasks include all sorts of things related to the image of the company.

Social media marketing is often a part of corporate marketing as well. You handle the Twitter and Facebook accounts, the Snapchat and Pinterest accounts—any channel the company may use. Social media marketing is a pretty complex job, and there are a lot of tools now—Hootsuite or Sprinklr or Tracx, among others—to manage your social media marketing presence.

In a lot of companies, it's hard to make MarCom accountable. Many other teams within the company, in fact, get frustrated because they view everyone to be measurable and accountable, except for MarCom. The more sophisticated startup CEOs that I know, however, put MarCom on a pretty tight measurement system. They set goals around how many leads come in through PR or social; how many articles are mentioned; how many visits come through the website through the articles, conversation rates; and other things of that nature. Any metrics you can put on MarCom are helpful, but typically it's trickier and more difficult to measure the impact of MarCom as opposed to other marketing roles. And there are times where you don't want to place too much emphasis on MarCom's metrics, which are sometimes referred to as *vanity metrics*—results that make everyone feel good because they're so visible, but don't actually correlate to the metrics that really drive up the value of the business.

In corporate marketing, writing skills are probably more important than anything else—you could be writing the press releases, the copy for the website, and any number of other kinds of communication.

Besides writing skills, it's vital to have good analytical skills, and to be very organized. When you're preparing to launch a product or pitch analysts, good organization is essential. You have to be a good project manager. Your job is to manage vendor relationships—for example, to select the PR firm (if you are hiring a PR firm—which most startups do although some prefer to handle press and media relations in-house) and to manage that relationship, or to select the design firm or website development shop and manage those relationships.

With such tasks, good interpersonal skills are also a must. Among the many relationships you focus on in MarCom, you'll be dealing with the press and analysts. Those relationships can serve a company very well in the hands of someone with strong interpersonal skills. You also have to be able to develop strong internal relationships with the parts of the organization that you interface most frequently with—Sales and Product in particular. And if you're doing event marketing, you have to be effective in getting people to show up, so being magnetic and charismatic is very valuable.

Product Marketing

As discussed, in chapter 2, there is a branch of marketing tightly linked to the product management function. However, while Product focuses on the internal, engineering-facing elements of the product, Product Marketing's role is to focus on its external, market, and customer-facing aspects. For example, Product Marketing thinks about a product's positioning and is responsible for watching the competition and being able to articulate how the startup's solution differentiates itself from the offerings of competitors.

At times, the product marketer will direct product managers and educate them on what's going on in the market, informing them of competitive trends, debriefing them on how the product is being viewed in the market. At other times, Product Marketing will take the direction of Product regarding priorities and messages. Importantly, Product Marketing is responsible for providing the sales team with the tools necessary to be effective in the field. Product marketers author all the communications with the sales team. They are often the ones writing the presentations and suggested scripts for the sales team. They also run sales training to train the salespeople on the product, the customer value proposition, and on how to sell the product.

In some startups, the product management teams will perform both the product management and product marketing functions until the company gets to a scale where they can afford separate functions. Once that happens, product marketing is typically more external and sales-focused and product management is more internal and engineering-focused.

As with other aspects of the marketing function, to do the product marketing job well, it's necessary to have good communication skills, to be a strategic thinker, and to have good analytical skills. You also need to be comfortable with technology, and you need to know the product well. Depending on how technical your product is, you want to be able to become a *power user* (an expert-level user) of the product—to know it better than the customer. You also want to know about your customers' environment, their needs, why the product addresses their needs, and what the competition's products are all about. Thus, you don't need to become a programmer, you simply need to be technical enough to *know the product*.

Interpersonal skills are important as well; in this role, you're constantly negotiating between Product and Sales.

Product marketers tend to have tremendous intellectual capacity and are often the most technical members of the marketing team. They have to think about competition and strategy and positioning, and they're attracted to all those things while also being able to communicate with the engineers. Because of this duality, one of my marketing friends refers to product marketers as "bilingual"— fluent in the language of both marketers and product engineers. Overall, they just need to be really human, to be service-oriented, and to recognize that salespeople are more important than they are, and they have to treat them as such—that their job is to make salespeople successful.

Some of the best product marketers I know treat the sales force like customers. Some of the worst product managers and marketers I know, on the other hand, are arrogant and think they're smarter than everyone because they're strategic and they know the product so well. They treat the sales team as being beneath them. This is no help to anyone.

It's a tough thing to be really strategic about your job and an intellectual leader—directing messaging and positioning—while also being able to put strategy aside and be service-oriented. But if you can do this, it will make you a great product marketer.

Demand Generation

Imagine how many times you have received a cold email or telephone call at home. It's annoying every single time, right? Trying to sell something by way of cold calls results in a very low hit rate. Compare that to watching an interesting webinar or responding to a piece of educational content like a downloadable white paper or compelling video. Suddenly, the person on the receiving end becomes a highly qualified lead, and you can hand that person over to a salesperson to set up a meeting, who can then have a much higher chance of closing a sale.

This is *demand generation.*

The demand-gen team is the very tightly measured group that generates leads for sales. They're in charge of the number of leads, number of demos, number of meetings that get set up—pretty much anything that helps the sales team. In a conceptual Venn diagram of sales on one side and marketing on the other, Demand-Gen lives at the intersection.

For a company to build a reputable, scalable sales and marketing machine, it has to have a great demand-gen engine. By generating awareness and getting highly qualified leads into the hands of the sales team, the demand-gen team gives Sales a running start in pursuing new opportunities.

Usually, either the demand-gen team or Product Marketing is responsible for responding to RFPs (requests for proposals), which a buyer uses to evaluate proposals from multiple vendors before buying a piece of software. In this role, your job is to answer the detailed product questions that the customer has to assist it in its evaluation process. Usually, someone on the marketing team, often demand-gen or product marketing, does the writing. Sometimes, Sales may quarterback the process, but they'll often still get a lot of help from the product marketing and demand-gen people.

In the demand-gen role, you're always thinking about how many calls you make per day to prospective customers. How many emails. How many conversions you had. How many demos you scheduled. How many people came to the webinar you were trying to recruit for. And what your conversion rate is—in other words, what happens to those leads after you toss them over to the sales team. You're always measuring the funnel and you're A/B testing and you're using tools like Google Analytics, Adobe Omniture, and Mixpanel and all sorts of other tools, where you're getting better and better at sophisticated measurement and analytics to drive marketing and inform possible marketing.

Some marketing departments have a role, often sitting within Demand-Gen, called Marketing Operations, or Marketing Ops. This role has been created because of all the data and systems coming out of marketing automation tools. Marketing Ops makes sure that the right leads are being transitioned to sales in the right way and that the sales reps are using the sales force automation systems properly and that they are integrated with the marketing automation systems. Marketing Ops might be the group that scores the leads, tracks them through the sales process, and does the win/loss postmortem analysis. Watching the data, making sure it is integrated across the organization, managing the marketing systems, and reporting cross-functionally on key marketing metrics are all the jobs of the marketing ops function.

You may have heard the term *nurturing* when it comes to leads. This is the idea of nurturing the interest of someone who has expressed curiosity about a topic. Let's say a person is exploring information around databases because she's developing a project for early next year that requires her to select one. At first, she's only interested in educating herself. She's in no rush—nothing is imminent. Why bother having a salesperson call her? It's not the time yet, and any insistence on your part could drive away the potential new customer.

Instead, you have a demand-gen person feed her new content every couple of weeks. Send her an article. Let her know there's a seminar happening in her region. Mention that there's a meet-up happening next week and offer a ticket. These actions nurture that lead and get her to the point where she's become highly qualified and ready to buy.

Ultimately, you need to be strategic about trying to lower the cost per lead, and to think about the value of a lead. It means being intellectually curious about what happened to those customers, and what the attributes are of the customers that tend to stick around year after year so you can try to attract more people like them. It means asking what you can do at the top end of the process to adjust customer retention in the future. That's what a good demand-gen person does.

It's an analytical job. It's thinking end to end.

Good demand-gen people also need to be very interpersonal, because they're trying to convince people to take meetings with salespeople. They're trying to convince people to convert—to get them down the funnel. Good listening skills are vital. You can't just have a script and rattle through it. You need to really listen to the customer—to ask, *What do you need? Where are you heading? What are the signals you're sending me?* and *How do I navigate our conversation to convince you that it's worth your time to take a meeting with one of the salespeople and learn more about our product?*

Acquisition Marketing

Many of the roles I have described above are relevant for start-ups that sell to enterprises. For startups that sell to consumers, the role of converting leads into sales may be done by a group in the marketing departments called Acquisition Marketing. This group tries to take all the leads and prospects and tries to get them to sign up for something or respond to something—ideally converting them into customers.

Codecademy, where I am an investor, is a good example of that.

Codecademy is an online service that teaches the world to code. It has a comprehensive set of interactive courses that it provides for free. Millions and millions of users have taken the courses and learned to code. The company also has a premium offering—a paid subscription product for $20 a month. You can get premium content access through your coding lessons and also a tutor or coach who can help you with coding. If you're using the free version of the service, you get none of that. The acquisition marketing team is responsible for trying to convert people to the premium model. They send emails, set up landing pages, and generally expose the Codecademy community to the paid product and try to convince them to take advantage of it.

In general, acquisition marketing involves a heavy amount of *content marketing*—the creation and distribution of relevant content with the aim of attracting and retaining qualified leads. Because of this, strong writing skills are again a must. Acquisition marketing is also very analytical. It's all about math—conversion rates, cost per lead, cost per install, cost per acquisition. It's all about cohorts (again, related data grouped for analysis). You need to be *hyper*analytical. You can have weak interpersonal skills, mediocre creative skills, and even mediocre strategic skills, but if you're extremely analytical, and you're always testing and running experiments and learning and adjusting and just being scientific about the process, you can be incredibly effective in customer acquisition. Of course, it still helps to be skilled in all these other areas; the point is simply that being analytical is *crucial*.

Community Management

In a world of viral marketing and social media, you want customers who will talk about you and recommend your product to others. An idea that has become powerful lately in StartUpLand is that of thinking of a startup's customers as a community. Customers who are part of such communities frequently serve as marketing agents, act as referring agents, and even solve each other's problems.

More than mere transactional users of your product, these customers are emotionally committed to your product and brand. For all those reasons, startups now often hire a community manager—someone who can create forums, send out a lot of the content, bring people together, run events, and create a sense of being a brand ambassador online.

For example, in our portfolio, we have a company called Jibo, which has built a "social robot for the home." We think a lot about Jibo's developer community, because we want developers to write applications on the Jibo platform. To that end, we've hired a community manager who is in charge of the software developer community. The community manager's focus is making sure that we're communicating with the developers effectively, and that they have the right materials and content to allow them to be successful. Codecademy has a community manager who focuses on the community of learners, pointing them to additional lesson plans they can work on to improve their coding skills. Our portfolio company, MongoDB, has a community manager who focuses on the MongoDB community and users, listening to them, making sure they're happy, and organizing their meetups. She's always chatting with members of the community online in the discussion forums—answering their questions, alerting them to new features, helping them solve each other's problems.

Whether it's in the context of a home robot, an online coding school, or an infrastructure software company, the community of users and developers plays an important function. It's the glue, so to speak, of the customer base, and it helps drive the goals I mentioned above.

All that rests on the community manager.

This role, like some of the other marketing roles, requires strong writing skills. Interpersonal skills are also crucial. As a community manager, you need to be charming and likable, and be able to develop a good sense of the sentiment of a community—to get people excited to use the product. You're a cheerleader, and an event planner. You're magnetic and charismatic.

You will also know the product really well. You can't be so high-level that you don't fully understand or appreciate the product. Some of the best community managers, in fact, come *from* the community themselves; they are the biggest cheerleaders because they are themselves power users or developers.

Erin Warren

Erin Warren, SVP of Marketing, Cartera Commerce

I was an Olympic luge racer in the 1994 and 1998 Olympic Games. That experience really taught me to be a self-starter and to be accountable for my own performance. I also learned how to work hard at something that very few people cared about because it mattered to me. That is really similar to being in a startup. If you work for a startup, you'll need to answer the "You work where?" and "What do they do?" questions so many times that you need to be confident in your own journey. It is just not as easy as saying, "I work at Verizon." And you need to be prepared to forge your own path. Luge racing at an elite level has prepared me well for that!

Having held leadership positions in both startups and large corporations, I think I have a unique perspective on the differences in these environments.

In larger corporations, you have access to resources (both internal and external) that you don't have in a smaller company. If you need particular expertise, you can acquire that knowledge/experience by bringing in experts or consultants. And when you have a much larger company, you typically have a broad knowledge base within your own employee base, which can take the form of having deep, specific expertise. Conversely, when you are at a startup, you often can't afford the luxuries of bringing in consultants. And when you are hiring for internal talent, you often need to recruit folks with a broader skill set so that they can respond to the twists/turns that a startup might require. Broad, adaptable folks tend to embrace the diversity of challenges that you can encounter at a startup.

That said, in a large company, there can be a level of abstraction on the overall business. Employees can feel disconnected from the overall goals of the organization, and functional leaders can build silos of expertise with goals that do not always translate well to the company's financial performance. Within the startup world, my experience has been that the employees are more in touch with the day-to-day performance of the company. And because there are fewer people and resources, employees need to work together to build the business. There is shared cross-functional purpose that drives directly to tangible business results. This is the heart of what makes a startup exciting for me.

Larger companies have time-worn processes that generally serve the needs of the company. Processes are well documented and play a critical role in the productivity of the workforce. Within a startup, change is inevitable and business growth is the primary objective rather than process efficiency. This can mean that process efficiency and communication are not favored as much as business-building progress. For those who require process and order, startup life can feel chaotic.

I think there are real benefits of both setups, and it has been rewarding for me to toggle between them. And I would encourage this as a career path that can be rewarding and inspiring.

PROFILE

Lynda Smith

Lynda Smith, VP Developer Strategy and Marketing, Jibo, and Lecturer, Stanford School of Engineering

I joined Jibo to structure and execute the developer program; Jibo is both the world's first social robot and a developer platform. As the role is defined today, I'm responsible for developer strategy and marketing, partner-related marketing, and corporate marketing. (A colleague has now taken over the consumer marketing efforts.)

So, in short, the role started off as all-around marketing support. In the first year, we accomplished the following:

- Go-to-market strategies for consumer and developer markets

- Brand development and implementation

- Messaging and positioning for company, product, and platform angles

- Crowdfunding campaign management

- Pricing evolution research and testing

- Community outreach strategy and management (including blog, social, and delivery communication components) for consumer and developer audiences

- Full-life-cycle customer experience mapping for consumers and developers

- Multichannel customer care/support strategy

- Developer SDK launch strategy and execution (including build out of developer portal, documentation, forum, etc.)

- Developer marketing plan and execution (including developer evangelism direction)

- Consumer launch strategy and pending execution (including PR, online content, social, advertising, and experiential marketing)

I'm a believer that marketing execs need to own the strategy piece as well as the tactics. Too often marketing is relegated to just being a tactical execution arm. It is also similar in that we are growing the marketing effort and introducing aspects that are part of the maturing process of a company. What is principally different is that we don't have a product in market yet. In my other positions, we had product. Software products are far easier to get into the market than hardware. And finally, this is the first company I've worked with that started as a crowdfunding initiative. This introduces a whole other level of marketing complexity.

Early in my career, I worked in large corporations, and what is different is the impact you can make in a startup. In the startup environment, you get to play in a lot of arenas, not all of which may be in your job description or even part of marketing. It's all hands on deck. You plug holes. You make things happen. And this is what I personally really enjoy.

I came to startups because I liked the visibility in the business you have in a startup and the level of control you have over a wide range of efforts. There is also an energy that comes with being in the startup world. It's about believing in the possible and being part of the team that is making it happen. There is also a great people dynamic that happens, especially if culture is taken seriously. The company becomes very much like family in that you are spending a ton of time together and having to deal with the good and the bad.

Attributes of a Strong Marketer

If we're looking for commonalities among the functions in StartUpLand, one of them is the ability to be a decathlete, not just a specialist who is awesome at the long jump or the shot put. It's somebody who can do it all without being dependent on teammates and to cover for them for various functions. The more multipurpose a person can be, the better.

Well, marketers are decathletes as well.

Beyond the attributes I've described within the individual roles, I think the best marketers at startups also have design chops and analytical chops. They collaborate on things, sure, but they're not dependent on other functions. They can get the work done themselves.

You also have to be a technophile. You don't want to have to go to the Engineering team for every little thing. You need to be able to use marketing automation tools, email marketing tools, A/B testing tools, analytics tools, and content management tools on your own.

This is how StartUpLand works. It requires a set of fundamental skills that are difficult to train in many ways. You need good writers and good communicators, but people who are also analytical and technical. You need strategic thinkers, but also people who are interpersonally strong and effective at tactical execution.

The work requires creativity in all forms. What's the joke you tell at the beginning of a phone call? What's the catchy thing you do in an email? What's the news snippet that you pick up? What's the emoji you throw in at the end of an email that gets people's attention, that makes them say, *Oh, this is a funny person. This is a human person. This is a likable person. This is a creative person. This is someone worth engaging with.*

Altogether, I realize, this sounds like somebody who is design-oriented while also being really technical and highly analytical. This combination of "left brain" (logical) and "right brain" (intuitive) attributes is a hard portfolio of skills to find, but people who can develop those skills are the magic of StartUpLand.

RESOURCES

For more about marketing roles and skills in StartUpLand, I recommend:

Books

- Shah, Dharmesh, and Brian Halligan. *Inbound Marketing* (Hoboken, NJ: Wiley & Sons, 2014). The two founders of HubSpot have written the seminal book on inbound marketing and demand generation.

- Scott, David Meerman. *The New Rules of Marketing and PR* (Hoboken, NJ: Wiley & Sons, 2015). This book provides a terrific review of modern marketing techniques across social and content marketing.

- Moore, Geoffrey. *Crossing the Chasm* (New York: Harper Collins, 1991). A classic book on marketing to early markets. Still regarded as the bible of startup marketing and market development.

5. **The Growth Manager**

In September 2012, Paul Graham of Y Combinator, a seed accelerator in Silicon Valley, wrote a provocative blog post titled "Startup = Growth" that shocked people. In it, he claimed that startups must grow an audacious 10 percent per week in order to be successful. Paul declared: "If there's one number every founder should always know, it's the company's growth rate . . . if you want to understand startups, understand growth."[1]

Let's do some quick math on that growth rate (which Paul did in his post). If you're growing 10 percent per week for an entire year, you will grow an astounding 142 times in one year.

Very, very few companies grow that much in one year, but Paul's point is an important one for anyone entering StartUpLand to internalize. Achieving growth is a core objective of most startup companies, whether that means growth in traffic, downloads, revenue—whatever. While in theory it is the responsibility of every function to contribute to the pursuit of this goal, in practice, every function has its own areas of focus that can sometimes distract from the overall goal of the company—driving growth.

In recent years, startups have decided that growth is such a central goal that rather than leave it to each part of the organization to execute on growth initiatives, they have started assigning individuals—and, at times, setting up entire departments—focused on growth. Sitting at the intersection of Marketing and Product, the growth function is focused on customer and user acquisition, activation, retention, and upsell. By viewing product development and marketing as integrated functions rather than as silos, companies are achieving breakthrough results.

This new role is often called the Growth Manager, Growth PM, Head of Growth, or Growth Hacker. In this role, you'll usually report directly to either the CEO or one of the executive team members, such as the Vice President of Product or Vice President of Marketing. You'll work with engineers, designers, analytics people, product managers, operations people, and marketing people to design and execute growth initiatives.

Growth has emerged as a new function because startups often value technical acumen and product design skills over traditional marketing expertise—a natural tendency, given the early-stage focus on searching for product/market fit in advance of scaling up customer acquisition and retention. In startups that have found product/market fit, optimizing growth becomes even more central.

At times, there can be organizational tension between Growth and Marketing or Growth and Product because of lack of clarity in role definition. Some startups encourage this tension because they want to create internal competition for the best ideas to surface, whether they originate from teams with a product-centric mindset or a growth-centric mindset.

The purpose of this chapter is to explain this new function as it is being pioneered by some of the fastest-growing, most innovative startups in the world. If you want to enter StartUpLand, you need to know what it's all about.

Functions of the Growth Manager

The growth manager's job has three core components:

- To define the company's growth plan
- To coordinate and execute growth programs
- To optimize the revenue funnel

To deliver on these core objectives, you'll have to take on several responsibilities.

Development of Data Systems

The fuel of the growth function is data. To get it, growth teams invest a significant portion of their resources to create the infrastructure that enables the analysis of user behavior, scientific experimentation, and targeted promotions. Measuring user experiences across product experiences and fragmented third-party systems (like advertising platforms, e-commerce systems, customer support interactions, and email marketing) is a challenge most companies face, and no other function is better positioned to coordinate the collection of the meaningful data streams than Growth. The data that flow from these systems serve the immediate needs of the growth team and are also provided as a shared service for other teams across the company ranging from product management to finance.

While many growth teams have special requirements that compel them to build their own custom data infrastructure, many work with commercial SaaS (software as a service) products. A number of popular data products are used by startup growth teams, including:

- *Web, mobile, and funnel analytics:* Adobe Analytics, Mixpanel, Google Analytics, Kissmetrics

- *Mobile analytics:* Flurry Analytics, Localytics, App Annie

- *A/B testing (also known as split testing) and personalization:* Optimizely, Maxymiser, Unbounce, Monetate, Visual Website Optimizer

Growth managers are typically responsible for selecting and integrating these products into the company's analytics framework and working either on their own or in partnership with the analytics team to provide dashboards and testing tools as services across the organization.

Defining the Growth Objective

A company's chosen growth metric is the most important metric around which to orient its priorities. It determines the most effective activities and, subsequently, the types of skills and resources you'll need on the growth team. Companies focused on user or customer acquisition generally tend to staff Marketing-led growth teams and tend to give more emphasis to the traditional demand-generation methods. More established startups tend to staff a Product-led growth initiative that focuses on making changes within the product to optimize user activation, retention, monetization, and upsell.

Once data is available to you in the growth manager role, you'll help the company answer two core questions. First, where should growth initiatives focus their resources across all the stages in the funnel from acquisition through retention and renewal? The answer to this question can be derived by analyzing customer behavior from top to bottom of the funnel, coupled with a thorough understanding of the product experience, usability, user perceptions, business model, and go-to-market strategy.

Second, what progress is the company making against its marketing goals? You'll help the company quantify and understand that progress by selecting a few important metrics—often called *key performance indicators* (KPIs)—and by developing reports for consumption across all of the teams accountable for growth initiatives. Some growth teams measure their company's performance against the absolute change in their selected KPIs. Since the overall performance of a business is affected by many external factors out of management's control, some teams choose another measurement method. They assess their direct contribution to growth by measuring the cumulative incremental improvements achieved against a given metric over the course of conducting tests that compare the results of a particular tactic to the baseline (i.e., A/B tests).

Customer Insight

The metrics you gather about customer and prospect behavior give an important view of customers, but it's an incomplete view. Data can reveal an underwhelming experience with the product in the market, but it can't usually show you what can be done to improve the experience. Actionable ideas come from a deep understanding of user needs, habits, and perceptions developed over time through targeted interviews, usability studies, and customer feedback. Growth managers analyze the data they pull from their data systems, in combination with qualitative analysis and user interviews, to answer some of the troubling "whys" that a company may have, such as:

- Why are users dropping out of the sign-up process?

- Why don't users come back to the application after the initial download?

- Why aren't users responding to special offers?

Growth can then feed these insights back to the product team to help them sort out product priorities, which impact the product roadmap.

Growth Product Roadmap Prioritization

The growth manager is responsible for prioritizing growth initiatives and product changes in harmony with the product manager. Ideas for initiatives to create growth originate in virtually all functions of the organization. As a growth manager, you are the champion for growth ideas, soliciting and evaluating suggestions from outside the growth team. Further, you must implement a framework for prioritizing growth-specific product improvements, and organizing the testing process. Generally, there will be more ideas than a team can implement, so the growth manager must apply both art and science to decide which changes are worthy of a test, and to balance the level of resources applied to a particular change as a result.

Sean Ellis, the founder of GrowthHackers.com and former Vice President of Marketing at LogMeIn, has a simple framework for prioritizing project ideas via ranking on three core measures (you can use a 1–10 scoring system or a high/medium/low label):

- A relative score of the impact of the change if it is successful

- A relative score of the confidence that this test will yield a successful result

- A relative score of the cost to execute the test

Taken together, these qualitative figures can help you negotiate amongst competing priorities within the pool of growth ideas.

Test Design and Implementation

With a clearly defined growth objective and prioritized roadmap of ideas to test, growth managers turn their attention to designing and implementing tests. If the test relates to a particular product, the growth manager leads a product development process to implement the change. The process often begins by writing a detailed Product Requirements Document (PRD) or creating a summary slide presentation that articulates the product changes needed. Next, the growth manager works with a cross-functional team, including engineering, analytics, design, marketing, and product to execute the test.

Growth teams can achieve significant efficiencies with various software analytical tools (including those I noted above) as well as by applying a range of programming tools that allow a non-engineer to address product flows, collect data, and analyze results without asking for resources and time from the engineering team. There is often a healthy tension between growth teams, who want to control tests directly that result in changes to the product and user flows, and the product team, who may have their own ideas about detailed product requirements and what should be tested. This tension is typically debated and resolved through a mix of data, negotiation, and the intuition of the most senior executive in charge of conflict resolution between Growth and Product.

PROFILE

Julie Zhou

Julie Zhou, Director of Growth, Yik Yak

I started my career in product and growth roles at Google and then at startups like Hipmunk and Yik Yak. At Yik Yak, Growth is product-driven: we own the user experience from the moment of app download until they become a long-term user. My team worked on projects like optimizing the onboarding process, increasing conversion to complete key actions, and sending personalized notifications based on user behavior.

In contrast, when working on growth at Hipmunk, my projects were marketing-driven and focused on making the top of the funnel bigger. Our top priorities were user acquisition, closing marketing partnerships, and increasing brand awareness overall.

To work at a startup, the absolute most important quality for a person to have is *drive*. He or she has to be driven every moment of every day to think of more ways that they can make the company grow, and then be driven to personally make those ideas happen. Because otherwise, chances are that task just will not get done. There is no one else to pick up the slack because there are so few people. They have to be driven to work fast and jump on new opportunities at a moment's notice. A startup's existence is dependent on finding product/market fit and building a sustainable business model before running out of resources. The competition always has more money, more manpower and more brand awareness than you do—what a startup has is single-minded focus on one goal and the drive to get there before anyone else does.

A startup is a completely different work environment to a corporate job like Google. The advantages that a startup has over a big company include: clearer focus (large companies tend to deal with infighting between teams working on different goals), nimble and efficient teams (you can spin up a new project in a matter of hours versus weeks), and a directly observable impact (it can be difficult to see how your work directly moves the needle at a large company). The disadvantages around startups are their emotional volatility (you will experience the highest of highs and the lowest of lows), the dependency on your relationships with coworkers (you'll be spending every working moment with the same group) and their inherent risk of failure (believe me, I know).

The Growth Function in the Context of the Company

Company Size

As with Marketing, a growth function tends to be created after a startup is already shipping its initial product and is in the early stages of achieving initial product market fit. That magic moment may come at twenty or thirty employees on the earlier side, or not until over a hundred employees on the later side.

Company size impacts both the organizational structure of the growth team and its interaction with other teams. In smaller companies, a single individual or a small growth team tends to operate as a shared service advising or coordinating the work of other teams. As an organization grows, it becomes more difficult to align disparate teams with the growth objective, and in these circumstances, the growth team is structured as a heavyweight team with all of its functions reporting to the same leader. Product teams are generally motivated to build features that add to the core value proposition before prioritizing features that contribute to the overall growth of the company. To manage the potentially conflicting objectives of growth and product development, some organizations temporarily transfer ownership of a product area to the growth team for a focused period of optimization. These kinds of temporary arrangements can create organizational tensions—sometimes purposeful, other times inadvertently.

At the Boston-based marketing software company Hubspot, the growth team was first created to develop and grow a freemium product line (i.e., free initial product, with additional charges as users need more features and capabilities) that helped promote the distribution of a new product offering. But after it was created, Hubspot's growth team ended up serving the broader organization: providing the guidance, measurement, experimentation, and reporting tools to enable product teams across the company to implement their own growth processes.

I know of a growth team at another prominent enterprise collaboration SaaS company that runs experiments across a small subset of its product customer base and uses the data that comes out of it to make recommendations to the core product teams. If the growth team finds something that can be improved, the product team implements the improvement within a given period of time across the entire customer base, even if it means adjusting the product roadmap.

Product Decision-Making Process

The product itself, and how people decide whether or not to use it, determines the set of viable growth methods and the company's approach to growth. For example, products that enable user collaboration and communication, such as LinkedIn, lend themselves to viral growth. Products used on their own or that involve multiple stakeholders in the decision-making process before they can be used, such as Amazon Web Services (AWS), will invariably require a different set of growth tactics.

Profit Formula

A startup's profit formula will help decide which growth methods it can use, and these in turn will determine how the growth team should be structured and what it will focus on. Companies without a proven monetization method will be loath to invest in channels where future returns are uncertain. Instead, they will tend to focus on growth methods that require minimal variable cost. For example, Airbnb has invested in a growth team that focuses on paid advertising (where profitability can be managed and measured), while another company, Remind—a text messaging application for teachers and students to communicate with each other—has yet to monetize and, instead, has been mostly focused on growing its user base in a sustainable, scalable way through unpaid channels like viral marketing (also known as *word of mouth* marketing).

Product/Market Fit Journey

Where a startup sits in its stage of evolution and journey toward achieving product/market fit will also shape the growth team. Companies that haven't yet found product/market fit are generally focused on iterating on the product, refining the value proposition while also searching for repeatable acquisition channels that attract customers who can give important feedback for improving the product. The growth team may be concerned about driving those acquisition channels—overlapping or replacing the marketing function, which may be more focused on MarCom and PR at this stage—or running well-structured acquisition experiments that will lead to discovering the most scalable acquisition method.

Once a startup finds product/market fit, the growth team will shift its focus to scaling acquisition and optimizing later stages in the funnel like user activation, engagement, retention, monetization, and renewal.

A cautionary word about growth teams at the earliest stages: *Be sure that they remain focused on sustainable growth and finding scalable sources of growth*—in other words, avoiding what one VC friend of mine refers to as "sugar highs" that provide a quick, short-term impact on a company's metrics but are not repeatable or sustainable.

Attributes of an Effective Growth Manager

Leadership and Culture

Leadership is an important attribute of the growth manager. You often sit outside the product team, but you need to influence it, as well as other leaders within the company, to achieve results. Larger companies that can afford multiple resources dedicated solely to growth may have an entire growth team. Within the team, you'll define the team strategy and priorities, facilitate collaboration between team members, modulate team morale and culture, advocate for resources, and liaise with executive stakeholders.

You'll also work with leaders of other market-facing functions on a shared growth objective. In some companies, other functions will look to your team for guidance on how to focus their efforts. Marketing, for example, might need input on which campaigns could earn the best results. Or a product team might want advice on how to improve the adoption rate for a new feature. Because you're often closest to the data about user behavior, and you sit at the intersection of user engagement throughout the entire funnel, you'll have unique insights into all of these questions.

At the same time, the growth team will depend on product teams to implement parts of the growth program. You'll work across teams to get buy-in for these efforts, and then drive action across teams.

A growth manager needs to be a leader in several ways: from people management, to creating alignment and accountability and providing motivation across teams, to managing upward and shaping ideas about the growth plan. It's up to you to get the team aligned, even in the face of uncertainty and doubt. Keeping the team focused on the highest-value activities is among the most challenging elements of the job.

The growth function can be fraught with failure, setbacks, and distractions. Your work might yield only small or temporary results, and you need to manage commitments, expectations, and morale—upward, outward, and within the team. Regardless of the team's structure, you'll inevitably depend on functions across the organization and you'll need to be able to influence teams without formal authority to recruit cooperation, resources, and support.

You also need to become a master of statistical reasoning, so that you can design effective experiments and develop an intuition for the user's experience. If data is the fuel of growth, then analytics are the engine. Over time, sophisticated analysis will help you develop your instincts, so you'll need to learn to understand and think through them. This means diving into the raw data and using tools like MySQL, Excel, the R programming language, and Tableau software to retrieve, manipulate, and visualize data.

In this role, you'll also become fluent in the full range of acquisition channels, like a marketer would be expected to be. James Currier, founder of Ooga Labs, identifies three general types of acquisition channels:

- *Owned media:* email, Facebook, Craigslist, Twitter, Pinterest, blog widgets, apps

- *Paid media:* ads (mobile, web, video, TV, radio, search engine marketing, affiliate), sponsorships

- *Earned media:* search engine optimization, public relations, word of mouth

Each of those channels has its own advantages, trade-offs, and idiosyncrasies. It's critical to have an intimate and specific knowledge of the tactics and techniques you can use in each channel to reach a product's target audience.

Many of the most successful technology startups have grown by scaling acquisition at very low cost by making use of viral channels. Airbnb, for example, famously built an unsanctioned Craigslist integration that allowed hosts to syndicate their listings to Craigslist for free. In this way, the company was almost immediately able to reach an existing audience of millions of target customers at virtually zero cost.

Early on, Eventbrite gained public awareness through the inherent virality that occurs when event organizers invite people to events. After attendees buy tickets, they learn that they can use Eventbrite to help organize their own events. This discovery delighted Eventbrite's early customers and solved some key pain points around their previous methods—pen and paper, spreadsheets, and manual collection of payments—all of which are terribly inefficient. More new event organizers invited more new event attendees, which triggered exponential growth. Over time, with a core service that solved a genuine problem for organizers of all shapes and sizes, the Eventbrite growth team optimized this natural virality to attain near-zero-cost customer acquisition.

An intuition for design, products, messaging, and marketing processes is also important for you in this role. Together, they enable you to effectively direct your cross-functional team and to create tests that will help you establish a compelling path forward.

The growth manager faces a lot of choices about where to focus precious labor and cash resources, so when formulating your strategic plan, it is important to understand and consider the operations of the company, the value proposition, and the profit formula. You'll learn to think like a CEO, and be able to make business model trade-offs in support of strategic priorities.

Methods and Best Practices

Although it's an evolving field, growth teams and managers go about achieving their objectives in the following ways.

One Growth Metric

First, a company needs an organizing objective that is easy to understand, universal, and clearly communicated. This one objective creates a shared context and language for every person in the organization to contribute to growth. Choosing a single objective can be challenging: the funnel is complex, teams have their own priorities, great ideas can come from various sources, and people work autonomously.

Alex Schultz, VP of Growth at Facebook, argues that, in the early days, companies should choose just one "North Star" metric. The CEO should establish this one metric and then measure progress against the goals set on it.[2]

The North Star should be chosen carefully to capture the internal performance of the funnel as much as possible. As discussed in chapter 4 (on marketing), many teams make the mistake of choosing a so-called vanity metric that gives them a false sense of success. Growth at the top of the funnel, for example, can be exhilarating, but true retention and conversion might suffer due to lack of product/market fit. The growth team at Pinterest uses "weekly active repinners" as their North Star, because they view pinning as a key indication of engaged users.

The Growth Model

As a business evolves, its growth plan will inevitably change. Part of evolving the growth objective for the company includes maintaining a current way of assessing performance at every layer in the funnel.

Growth teams often maintain a working model of the dynamics in the business that is updated manually or algorithmically on a regular basis. The model is often a simple waterfall chart of user activity at all of the meaningful milestones between the top of the funnel and churn (e.g., a hundred people visit the website, twenty people register, ten people activate, and two people pay) with additional dimensions superimposed (geography, acquisition source, etc.).

Matt Boys, former Growth Marketing Manager at payments startup Stripe, uses a model like this to stack rank from highest to lowest areas of investment, then chooses a stage and a growth metric suited to that stage, and dedicates a period of time to running experiments focused on improving just this metric.

New-User Experience

Growth teams hoping to optimize conversion from acquisition to activation will focus on improving a user's first interactions with the product to remove a customer's hurdles to adoption of the product, deliver meaningful value, and explain the value proposition. UX professionals often know a lot about this area and can help craft and test design flows that maximize adoption.

The growth team at Pinterest was able to increase new user activation by more than 20 percent with an increased flow of new users. The company changed its onboarding experience from a text-intensive explanation of the concepts in the service and a generic feed of the most popular content to a visual explanation and personalized content feed based on a survey of user interests. As a result, the team was able to better explain the value proposition and to train the user—all of which ultimately led to better conversion from acquisition to activation.

By comparing behavior of the users who continued logging back in versus those users who stopped using the service (i.e., churned out), the early Facebook team determined that a key driver of new user retention was finding and connecting with at least ten friends within the first two weeks after signup. With this in mind,

Facebook developed features to allow users to quickly see and connect with friends who were already using the service.

Cohort Analysis

As is the case for the marketer, cohort analysis is a fundamental tool for the growth manager. Growth teams need to measure the company's progress toward the startup's key objectives over time and watch over the relative performance of different flows in the design to identify opportunities for optimization. However, it's next to impossible to accurately quantify the impact of every improvement a company makes to its product and go-to-market processes over time. It can take a long time for the impact to be realized, and it is unfeasible to A/B test every change being made.

Thus, cohort analysis is a great tool for watching trends in overall company performance and spotting suboptimal product experiences. In order to measure a given dimension, such as signup period or acquisition source, users can be segmented into groups and the measurable behaviors of each group (activity, conversion, revenue, etc.) can be compared as a function of time since acquisition. The customer's tenure matters because you are often trying to project attrition rates over many months or even years by extrapolating the behavior you observe during the few months or even weeks that you have collected user data. Startup executives have the general challenge of making decisions based on limited data, and time is often the greatest limitation.

Product Positioning

Most products offer an array of value propositions, so conversion across stages in the funnel is a function of how well users understand the specific jobs that a product can perform for them. Growth teams dedicate considerable effort to running tests and refining the explanation of product benefits. This is an ongoing process that evolves with product development as new insights emerge as to how users are deriving value from the product.

The growth team at Pinterest increased its signup conversion rate by making improvements to messaging on the Pinterest landing page. The team started with the hypothesis that messaging focused on specific-use cases would more concretely demonstrate the value of the service and thereby entice more people to sign up. The team A/B tested five different designs. Four of them performed worse than the existing landing page. The fifth, which featured several different but distinct gender-neutral-use cases (hobbies, travel, cooking, etc.), improved performance by 15 percent.

Matching the Growth Goal and Activities

The mix of tactics that the growth team chooses must be compatible with the magnitude of the growth objective and the company's horizon for growth. The finite reach of each stage in the funnel means that there is a limit to how much growth can be achieved through optimizations. Growth in excess of what can be achieved by optimization requires the development of new acquisition channels. Further, the focus of growth activities should also match the time horizon for growth, which is generally a function of the company business plan. Driving near-term sales would shift focus toward prospects lower in the funnel (e.g., driving demo requests), while a longer-term scaling plan would compel the growth team to focus on improvements that take longer to bear fruit but could have a larger overall impact (e.g., search engine optimization and content, brand, and community). Activities must match the size and type of growth desired.

Rapid Prototyping

Product development in service of growth should be lightweight, rapid, and iterative. Predicting the success of a given change is difficult; hence, product improvements should not be over-engineered.

Many companies will target minimally viable product improvements until a particular method is proven to be fruitful. Most experiments fail to produce significant impact, so the odds of discovering a successful change is aided by a short experiment cycle time. Executing such a process can be difficult.

Growth managers work to build a culture that values the quick and insightful over the beautifully designed effort. They also diplomatically manage relationships and communications internally; for example, when a test reflects poorly on a product owned by another team. And growth managers need to coach their team of engineers and designers to tolerate the frustration of watching their work get discarded when it proves ineffective.

Usability Testing

Armed with the right data, the growth manager can become a champion for users across the organization. The *usability test* is one of the best methods for developing empathy and insight into a company's target users. There are many ways to conduct usability tests, from setting up a complete testing lab to doing ad hoc guerrilla testing at a coffee shop. Services like UserTesting (usertesting .com) make it easy to run quick, lightweight tests on a target demographic of users.

Barry Malinowski, Growth Product Manager at education service Udacity, ran online usability tests in which test participants compared a prototype Udacity homepage design variation to competitor homepages. Because the study was anonymous, Malinowski was able to get an unbiased, qualitative comparison to competitors and then generate ideas for improving Udacity's design.

Segmented Feature Development

While broad improvements to a product that affect all users typically yield the most positive results, there can be significant value in focusing on a specific subset of users. Many growth managers will thus focus on building targeted features to suit the needs of a focused community of users to acquire new customers and generate positive word of mouth.

The team at Wealthfront, an automated wealth management service, built a specific feature to help employees of companies with a recent IPO (initially, Facebook and Twitter employees) transition to a diversified portfolio. While Wealthfront aims to be a generic service used by millions of people, employees with new wealth generated in an IPO stand to uniquely benefit from the service. This IPO feature for this valuable client segment makes it easy for new customers to transition to Wealthfront, and also helps the Wealthfront team convince these companies to promote its service to their employees.

Comparison with Product and Marketing

Many startups struggle with how growth differs from the product or marketing function. Because it is such a new function, and because the points of overlap are somewhat intentional to create internal tension, the confusion is understandable. Table 5-1 may help sharpen the distinctions between the functions.

TABLE 5-1

Growth function compared with Product Management and Marketing

	Product	Marketing	Growth
Mission	Solve customer problems	Communicate differentiated value	Run growth experiments
Focus	Direct engineering to deliver product that meets customer requirements	Support sales to drive revenue	Increase market share by finding repeatable acquisition techniques
Rallying cry	Ship!	Promote!	Grow!

Becoming a Growth Manager

Because it is a relatively new role and requires an integration of many skills, there are many paths to becoming a growth manager in StartUpLand. One of my former students runs Growth at a hot payments startup. He was an economics and philosophy major in college, and upon graduation, joined a large technology company as an analyst. This role provided him with a great background for Growth because he became close to the data and was able to see the implications of changes in a product or service reflected in the data. Former product managers or marketers might also be converted into the growth function. Good growth managers are highly analytical, deeply technical, and excellent communicators. If you can blend those attributes, you can become a terrific growth manager.

The growth manager function is still evolving, but it's become an indispensable engine for many technology companies. If you like a diverse set of responsibilities and have a passion and knack for analytics, marketing, and product development, you can thrive in this role.

RESOURCES

For more about growth roles and skills in StartUpLand, I recommend:

Books

- Ellis, Sean, and Morgan Brown. *Hacking Growth* (New York: Crown Business, 2017). This book provides a detailed review of the growth role and numerous case studies of growth efforts, written by a leading practitioner in the field.

- Holiday, Ryan. *Growth Hacker Marketing: A Primer on the Future of PR, Marketing, and Advertising* (New York: Portfolio, 2014). A popular writer in tech and business,

Holiday digs into how Facebook, Uber, Dropbox, and Airbnb have executed their growth campaigns.

Other Resources

- *GrowthHackers* (blog). www.growthhackers.com. This blog provides a rich set of projects, blog posts, and a network of fellow growth managers to learn from and collaborate with.

6. **Sales**

A VP of Sales in one of my portfolio companies used to say, "I'm simply a pie salesman."

After hearing him say it a few times, I finally asked, "What do you mean?"

He said, "I drive the truck in the morning. I pull over. I open up the back of the truck and I look at what pies I have in the truck. If I have blueberry pies, then that day I'm selling blueberry pies. If I have apple pies, then that day I'm selling apple pies. I don't try to sell what I don't have, because if I try to sell what I don't have, I'm going to be in trouble. People are going to be unhappy with me, so I've simply got to sell what's in the truck."

I've always liked that metaphor because it's so simple and honest. Software can be so complicated, so full of features and functionality. Basically, you have to be able to sell what's in the truck. The job is that simple.

Salespeople are the first line of gathering information about market requirements. They talk to customers every day and listen to what the customers' needs are, what problems they're trying to solve. Salespeople watch their customers' environments, keep track of what the competition is doing, and stay on top of industry trends.

In a big company, this information often is ignored by the executives and corporate staff sitting at headquarters; it just goes in one ear and out the other. Venture capitalist Lars Dalgaard tells the story of when he transitioned from Sales to headquarters at a *Fortune* 100 pharmaceutical company and found out that a voice mail box containing feedback from the field had not been listened to in years. "When I sat down to listen to them, there were almost ten thousand messages!" In a small company—in a *startup*—this feedback represents incredibly valuable information. Salespeople can bring it back into the company and use it to strategize with the leadership people and with Product and Engineering to describe what's going on out there in the field.

I believe deeply that Sales is a very noble endeavor and a worthy place for people to start their careers. If you are looking to join a startup and have the grit and determination to succeed, Sales is a great entry point. First, it's a fantastic way to learn and to build your career close to the revenue, close to the customer. You're accountable to a number, so it offers a clear-cut way to track your successes and develop a track record of hitting your goals. Anytime you want to rise up in any organization, that closeness to the revenue and crisp accountability is invaluable.

The core function of a company is to earn profit by solving customer problems by providing valuable solutions. This is what salespeople do literally every day. If the salesperson is successful, the company is successful—because the salesperson's activities are so precisely tied to revenue generation.

In no other function is the impact of your work so obvious. When you're in Marketing, Engineering, Product, even Finance, your outcomes are usually a little fuzzier, and it can be unclear how you directly contribute. These roles have a lot of intangibles. Sales is *very* tangible and *very* directly linked to the success of the company. The measurement of the sales team is how much revenue or bookings you bring in relative to your designated quota. The measurement of the accounts team (part of Sales) is renewal achievement. Everyone in Sales knows the score every day.

In that capacity, you can build incredibly valuable skills and experiences.

The Sales Role

No matter what technology you're talking about, even in premium models, at some point, somebody needs to sell it. The sales process could be telephone-based sales. It could be email-based sales. It could be heavily marketing oriented in terms of content marketing, pushing a lot of content out there to get people engaged to get demos done. At some point, somebody needs to sell.

Let me tell you the story of Dropbox.

Dropbox is the perfect viral product. If I have a file I want to share with you and choose Dropbox as the tool to share it, you have to set up a Dropbox account in order to receive it.

At first, I thought Dropbox would sell itself. People would hit the limit of memory that came with the free account and then want to buy the premium version. And that did happen (and still does). Then, a few years after the company started, one of my students went to work there and they asked him to create a sales force. He and I talked about it, and I began to realize that although a lot of people were getting the free product, there was an opportunity for Dropbox to be more proactive in reaching out to its happy customers to convince them to upgrade to the paid version—an opportunity to reach out to corporations and convince them to adopt the product more broadly within the company.

Fast-forward a few years, and my student had created a hundred-plus-person sales organization. Today, Dropbox's sales organization does enterprise selling and telephone-based selling and works with channel partners throughout the globe.

As soon as a company decides it wants to make money— something all companies need to do at some point—it needs to come up with a revenue or monetization strategy. To maximize revenue, a company needs to reach out to prospects, pilots, and— in some cases—free users and say, *Hey, I notice your customer needs are . . . And you seem to have liked and used that free product. You would probably benefit from our paid product. Here's why. Here's the value proposition.*

That's startup selling. And it's a big subject. In this chapter, I break it into as many pieces as I can so you can see how each role works and how they relate to each other.

To start, sales organizations fall into two main types: outside sales, often called field sales, and inside sales.

Field Sales

The field salesperson is a very important person—a high-impact individual—because this role is one of the core revenue generators for a company. Without salespeople to close deals, there is no revenue.

As the field salesperson, also sometimes referred to as the *outside salesperson*, you're sort of the BPOC—the big person on campus. You're the one bringing in the big deals, and the whole company is hanging on them. Others will ask what they can do to help you, whether or not the product needs to change, whether the CEO needs to fly across the country to meet with the customer, whether the CTO can help answer a prospect's technical questions. They'll ask if the marketing team needs to pitch in to answer an RFP, and if the service team needs to show up to talk about an implementation plan. It's an empowering role, because you're the hero. You're in front of customers all the time, pushing, selling, advocating. Then you bring in the contract, slap it on the table, and everybody cheers.

Field sales typically involves heavy travel, which can have great appeal. If you're in a New York–based company, you might have an office in New York, but also offices in San Francisco and London. Over time, a field person gets hired in those offices and needs to cover large geographic territories. For example, many of my early startups hire one sales rep for the entire western part of the

United States out of the San Francisco office and all of Europe out of the London office.

As an outside salesperson, you can make great money if you hit your quarterly goals. Besides your base salary, there are on-target earnings. So you might make a $100,000 base and another $100,000 in target-earning bonuses, because you're bringing $1.5 million into the company in high gross margin revenue every year. If you exceed your target, you can make $300,000, or $400,000, or $500,000. Sometimes, the outside salesperson is the highest-paid executive in the company. Although you don't get as much equity, you can frequently make more than the CEO.

The downside of being a sales rep is that your job is on the line every quarter. If you miss your number once, you get a warning. Twice and you're fired. It's that cutthroat. As a sales rep, when you close the sale and make your number, you celebrate. When you blow the sale or it goes in another direction, you're screwed. Salespeople compete and win or lose every quarter, and their numbers show it.

Some people like the risk/reward roller coaster. Sales is a bit like having the ball at the end of a basketball game, down by one, and you're the one taking the final shot as the clock winds down. It's a make-it-or-miss-it kind of job. So it's not for everyone. Others like to be more operational, more in control of their day, more steady, with fewer highs and lows.

That's the dynamic.

Field salespeople tend to have a dramatic flair. As a field salesperson, you interact with customers directly, often face to face, are often traveling, located frequently in remote offices (even in the internet age, buyers often like to meet real people to make their buying decisions). These buyers tend to represent larger sales opportunities—at least $50,000 or more. Often, annual contracts will amount to $100,000 or more, and these deals tend to be a little more complex.

Occasionally, people will tease salespeople by saying derogatorily that they're "coin-operated." It means you can just keep telling them what to do, and as long as you put money in the slot, they'll keep doing it. You put the coin in the machine and you pull the lever, and the thing spins. As a field salesperson, you hit your goal, make money, and help the company be successful. In truth, the best salespeople are more sophisticated than that stereotype. The best ones, in my experience, are strategic thinkers on behalf of the customer and love solving their problems and helping them become successful (in fact, there is a particular sales technique, where the salesperson focuses on addressing a customer problem more generally rather than just pushing a particular product, known as *solution selling*). Further, effective salespeople are great listeners, and that doesn't just benefit the customer: the insight a salesperson brings back to the company is invaluable. Some companies find the sales team's insights so valuable that they ask a salesperson to represent the voice of the customer in product review meetings.

But ultimately, a salesperson is laser-focused on driving revenue day in and day out, and good salespeople are very effective at avoiding any distractions and removing any obstacles that get in the way of achieving revenue targets.

When people want me to hire them into sales functions, the first thing they always talk about is their achievement against their quota during the last few years: *I was 115 percent of quota in 2016. I was a member of the President's Club. I was the top rep in the United States. In 2014, I was 105 percent of quota. In 2015, I was 118 percent of quota.* It shows that there was a goal, and that they achieved the goal. The next year, they set another goal, and achieved that goal. And on and on.

The other thing a lot of salespeople are very proud of is being a part of the revenue growth of a company over time. You'll hear a lot of: *I was the VP of Sales, or the Director of Sales, or the Head of Inside Sales at a company that went from $1 million in revenue when I joined to $20 million, then to $100 million in revenue. I was a part of that journey of a twenty-times or hundred-times growth curve over the last five years.*

I know CEOs and Sales VPs who, in board meetings, will purposely orchestrate things so they can interrupt the board meeting with the news that a big deal has been signed. They walk in and they'll say, *Hey, I'm sorry to interrupt the meeting. I just have some great news. We just closed a deal with Kraft for $600,000.* Everybody celebrates, claps, and high-fives. They'll try to create a sense of drama and excitement, right in the board meeting.

My favorite tactic is when the CEO is presenting to the board, and the VP of Sales will turn to the CEO and cut in and slyly say, *I haven't even updated you on this yet,* then rattle through a few positive conversations from the last twenty-four hours: *We just got the signature on the deal with Disney. The verbal from Goldman Sachs came in an email while I was sitting here.* Months and months of effort by some individual sales representative, in coordination with the entire executive team, went into that sale. And when it comes through, there's nothing like that feeling of team success.

This dynamic is why former athletes are frequently drawn to sales. There's a scoreboard, and the scoreboard is very clear at the end of the day. The job is all about keeping your stats, hitting your numbers, working as a team, and winning.

At Upromise, we hired Dave Ponder, a former Dallas Cowboys lineman, into our sales organization. Ponder was 6'3" and probably played close to 300 pounds. When he walked into a conference room, he was literally a really big presence. Everybody wanted to talk to him about what it was like in the NFL, what it was like playing for the Cowboys, about his teammates, and so forth.

With all this small talk and sports talk, the client prospects would get warmed up and build a nice relationship with Dave. Then he would get down to business and talk about why they should partner with Upromise and do business with us. He was a killer sales executive because he had that affable personality and exciting backstory combined with a competitive instinct and hard-work ethos. But beyond the personal attributes, Dave was a successful sales executive because he took the time to understand our company, our value proposition, and how it might meet the needs of our target customers. He truly cared about the customers being successful with our service, and it showed.

That's field sales.

PROFILE

Ahron Oddman

Ahron Oddman, Regional Sales VP, nCino

Working at a startup is a transition for me from the Marines, an organization of over two hundred thousand. In the Marines, I was many layers of management removed from an executive who had the authority to make consequential decisions, especially concerning how to deploy our capital or talent. I was often frustrated by this experience. At my current company, my experience is exactly 180 degrees out. I often travel and collaborate with the CEO during sales cycles.

My boss reports directly to the CEO and I talk to my boss three to four times a week. In addition, my CEO has cleared everyone in the company to act autonomously and to spend resources if it's in the best interest of a customer.

All of our sales representatives have the responsibility to drive revenue with new and existing customers, but also are required to do much more. They sit on product stakeholder committees to inform our product managers of customer feedback, help develop market collateral and presentations, and speak at industry conferences.

At large organizations, initiative will set you apart. At a startup, it is a prerequisite. In the Marine Corps, if you displayed initiative, your personal brand would rise, you'd be applauded and rewarded with more work, but not more authority. At a startup, it is table stakes to display large amounts of initiative, and you have to be comfortable doing it in gray areas. You must be OK with being wrong.

The "professional risks" of joining a company that could fail don't stand as a deterrent from joining a startup and operating in the gray.

Many of us conflate things that are *scary* (flying in combat, joining a startup, buying a company) with things that are *dangerous* (not preparing before a flight, working in a setting that isn't fulfilling because you want safety). Many things that aren't scary are in fact dangerous. Joining a startup that is serving a constituency you care about, systematically pursuing product/market fit, and one in which *you* can contribute to is scary, but it's not dangerous.

PROFILE

Thomas Howe

Thomas Howe, Sales Representative, Google Enterprise

When I joined Google Enterprise, we were a startup within a big company. Now, we have five products we sell to corporations. My responsibilities are to identify opportunities within *Fortune* 1000 accounts, qualify them, position Google tech, and close them.

I started my career at a big company. Then I went to Information Builders and Sybase, which were medium-sized companies. I then joined a startup right after its IPO.

I've spent over ten years at startups. I wanted the potential economic upside (the equity payday), and I liked the ability to stick my fingers into a lot of different functional areas within the startup (Marketing, Finance, Product Management, etc.). I personally get fairly jazzed about elegant tech and the potential to create a whole new market or participate in a seismic shift, like e-commerce or cloud computing at Google. That desire really acts as a primary driver.

The startup environment is substantially different—in a good way. Large companies tend to be stodgy, bureaucratic, slow-moving, and frugal. They are also safe (maybe less so nowadays), but safety has never been something I've focused on. Startups are much more collaborative; lots of people give advice outside of their area of responsibility. Large companies are beset with finger-pointing and politics. This is much less true at startups. Startups are more nimble and, due to their smaller size, there tends to be less red tape.

The big difference between the large companies and the startups is the available resources. You take things for granted at big places—things like marketing, administrative help, databases (corporate data on prospects like org charts, names, and contact info), brand recognition, and resources in general. Then you get to the startup and start asking for things and realize, *Geez, I'm going to have to do all of this from scratch.*

Many times at a startup, you feel like a lone wolf—out on your own, trying to succeed with sparse resources. Because you don't have those resources at a startup, you also have to dive in and understand the tech fairly well in a very short amount of time. So having a good technical knowledge base is an asset for sales reps. You also have to be a self-starter. If you're used to having people give you tasks and tell you what to do and when to do them, you're going to struggle at a startup.

I have always gotten a kick out of watching a new customer take my tech and create something wonderful that's helped them save money, or make more money, or come up with new products. That drive to see how my products can fundamentally remake a *Fortune* 500 account is definitely a passion that pushed me to join startups.

I like the risk/reward trade you find at startups. Startups are like a breath of fresh air. The environment is exciting and dynamic, and everybody is enthused and invested.

There's nowhere to hide, so everyone plays a vital role and there is a collaborative spirit in a startup. There's also a much higher sense of urgency. Sales at a startup are met with enthusiasm and celebration. When business comes in the door, nobody takes it for granted.

Inside Sales

Growing in strategic importance and emphasis at startups, the inside sales job is very different than field sales. Inside salespeople (also sometimes called *business development representatives* [BDRs]* or sales development representatives [SDRs]), are typically at their desks all day, on the telephone and pounding out emails. It's a job characterized by a tightly defined process. The inside sales reps are measured by how many calls per day they're making, how many emails they're sending, how many demonstrations they've given, thus measuring their customer activity in whatever way it is appropriate for the business.

I was meeting with one of my companies recently, and was told proudly, "We've got this new dialer technology. We have an outside company make all these phone calls because it's so hard to get people on the phone. As soon as a person answers a call, our sales rep's headset lights up and connects. Our salespeople don't have to waste time dialing and leaving messages. It just happens automatically. As soon as a live person picks up the phone—boom, they're on. Anything to make the sales rep's time more efficient."

Inside sales is often thought of as more of an entry-level position. Salespeople in this role are typically younger and are typically paid

---

*The common term *business development representatives*, or BDRs, is distinct from the business development function described in chapter 3. The former is a junior sales support resource, whereas the latter is a more senior executive role that sits outside of sales. This confusion is why many prefer to use the acronym BDRs or its sister term, *sales development representatives*, or SDRs.

less than field sales reps. Sometimes they're right out of college or only a few years out of school. Sometimes it's their first job.

A firm in Boston, LaunchSource, provides training and placement into startups for recent college graduates to become inside salespeople. Right out of college, you get trained for a month, and LaunchSource will then feed you into a fast-growing, exciting company. These companies hire dozens—sometimes hundreds—of inside salespeople who sit in cubicles, lined up on the phone, shooting out emails, learning how to sell. The BDR or SDR role is at the center of the revenue generation process for these companies. Those sales representatives are sometimes outbound oriented (i.e., they make outbound calls or send emails to prospects) or inbound oriented (i.e., they react to inbound inquiries or expressions of interest).

For example, if the marketing team does its job, strong content may be put out there in the form of a white paper. The white paper is promoted using the company's social channels. Let's say that Sally, a prospect, clicks on it, fills out a form, and downloads it. As soon as that happens, an inbound sales representative gets an email alert and can respond quickly: *Hi, Sally, I noticed you downloaded a white paper about our voice collaboration software. We'd love to tell you more about it. Can I set up a demo? Can I plug you into a webinar we're holding next week, featuring our founder? Would you like to attend an event that we're holding in your city? Would you like to talk to one of our customers to hear how they're using our system to become more efficient?*

All these tactics are aimed at drawing leads in and moving them down the funnel of awareness, consideration, engagement, intent, and (hopefully) purchase.

Some sales organizations are structured so that the inside salesperson's job is strictly to get meetings for the outside salespeople. Your job is to do the research and networking to find potential buyers, contact them, get them interested in learning more, and then convince them to set up a meeting: *One of my colleagues, Marcie, is going to be in Nashville on Monday. She would love to come visit you to continue the conversation and give you an opportunity to learn more about our product.*

Then Marcie scrambles her schedule so she can show up in Nashville and visit with that lead.

That's the inside sales job.

As they get older, more experienced, and more successful, inside salespeople sometimes graduate to become field salespeople or account managers. Others become successful at inside sales and then become inside sales managers. They move up the chain—to manager, then maybe to a director position, or maybe the VP of Inside Sales. Over time, some become VPs of Sales, Chief Revenue Officers, and eventually maybe even CEOs.

Others go into Product or Marketing. Through a couple of years in sales, you can gather a lot of market intelligence and insight, so the product leader might come to you and say, *Hey, now that you know the product so well, I'd love to have you come in as product manager. You've learned the value proposition. You've learned about our customers. Now come help us shape the product to be a better fit for them.*

Because the business models are so varied, salespeople in start-ups don't need to be traditional, briefcase-carrying, blue-suit-red-tie salespeople. Some people wonder if they need to be slick car-salesman types and glad-handers in order to succeed in Sales. The answer is no. You can be a cerebral, strategic, thoughtful, introverted person and be a *fantastic* salesperson. You just have to pick the type of business model that is conducive to that.

Maybe you want to be behind the screen, and maybe you'd rather interact with people through email and chat than in person. A lot of sales tools today are chat-based. When you go on to an e-commerce website, what happens if you linger on that site? A "Live Chat" box pops up and a salesperson or customer service representative is on the other side of the chat: *How may we help you today? How can we help you? Hey, Robert, I saw you looking at the pants. Is there a particular style that you liked? Can I help you find something? Do you want a belt with that?*

Inside salespeople collaborate with the product management team to think about ways to use the design of the product to convert you from free to paid service. They think about how to maximize the average revenue per user.

Consider the information software company Mattermark, for example. First, you sign up for its free newsletter and receive insightful information in your inbox about startups and financings. Then, to get access to more detailed information about private companies and import that information into Excel, you might sign up for a fourteen-day free trial. You fill out the online form and are immediately able to access Mattermark's rich information database and integrations. On day 13 of your free trial, there's an email in your inbox: *Hey Jeff, I see your free trial is about to end. Would you like to sign up for our $200-per-month Individual Plan? Or are the features of our $500 per month Professional Plan more appropriate given how you're using the product?* On day 15, if you don't reply to that initial email, your phone rings. That's an inside salesperson.

As mentioned earlier, in small companies, Product, Marketing, and Sales are typically in direct, frequent contact. Again, this is a big difference between big companies and small companies. The bureaucracy is eliminated in a small company. People talk to each other all the time. You're in an open floor plan, so you can't help but talk to each other. So Product says, *What happened yesterday when you spoke with Pepsi? How did that demo go? Oh really? They asked for that feature? You heard that one of our competitors responded in a different way and that the price was different than our pricing structure? That's really interesting. Let me take that back and think about that.*

It happens all the time.

Sales is about identifying a customer's pain point, articulating a value proposition that solves that pain point, giving people a call of action, conversion, and ultimately driving revenue. You're trying to do this whether you're flying around the world to meet prospects eyeball to eyeball or hitting the phone lines.

Sales Engineers

The sales engineer (SE) is the wing person for the salesperson, sitting between the engineering organization and the sales organization to provide greater technical expertise and to interface with customers who may be more technical and who need more specific assistance than a typical salesperson can provide. They often do the demos for customers. They also often set up the prototypes to be used in the demos.

There is often a ratio of one SE for every two to four field sales reps and one SE for every four to six inside sales reps. Sales reps will do their work to develop a relationship, establish a need and opportunity, and have an initial meeting or two before they ask the SE to join on a sales call. The sales rep's follow-up meeting might include the customer's IT director or chief architect or CTO. Those people are likely to ask a bunch of technical product questions. The SE can help address those questions.

As you might guess, the SE often either has a technical background or is technically savvy enough to go toe-to-toe with a technical customer. But an SE's knowledge base is different from that of a product manager in that SEs need to be able to talk about more than just a product component or even the entire product. They may talk about the whole *suite* of products and how the products fit into the customer's environment. It means being an expert in how customers use the product and how they might integrate the product or the suite of products into their environments. The difference between what they need to know and what the product manager needs to know is subtle, but it is an important distinction.

Many SEs, as they get more senior, may end up going into either Product or Direct Sales (outside sales), depending on whether they enjoy the technical and product aspects of the job more or whether they enjoy the selling and the interpersonal interactions more.

The SE role is a great entry-level position for someone who is technically minded and who maybe has a degree in computer science, physics, or engineering. If you like hacking and playing around with technology, maybe enjoy coding but are not necessarily interested in becoming a software developer, and would prefer to interact with people more and travel a bit, the SE role is a good fit.

SEs are really good at explaining technical things clearly. If you identify with this statement and think it sounds too easy, you should know that few people do this exceptionally well (engineers, for example, aren't always so great at it). This skill can make you an invaluable resource on a sales team. Besides manifesting the concepts and the code, you'll have the constant challenge of articulating a product's value proposition and technical features and functionality in a clear fashion. It's as if you have a software developer's product and technical knowledge with a salesperson's personality.

Sales engineers also often become industry analysts. I have worked with sales engineers who later joined companies like Forrester and Gartner. After going into customer environments for a while within an industry, and writing and presenting about that industry along the way, it's a natural evolution to want to analyze the whole sector as opposed to working for a single company, selling a single product.

Personality-wise, sales engineers are nerdy. They like new things. They like prototyping and trying things out. They're early adopters. They're good communicators and good presenters, and are good on their feet in sales situations while getting barraged with tough and sometimes even hostile questions. Selling to technical customers can be challenging, and SEs need to handle the process graciously and patiently.

You might go visit a customer to do a demo, for example, when a customer says, "This is totally incompatible with our systems and would never work in this environment." You need to be able to say, "It actually can be very compatible." And then explain how. A customer might question whether or not you have examples of companies using the product well. You need to be able to show those examples. When a customer says the examples are in a different industry, and that their systems are far less complex than the customer's, you need to be able to present information that speaks to their concerns and guide them toward a feeling of trust (assuming your product actually can, in fact, do what the customer needs).

This challenging dynamic happens all the time for sales engineers. It's important to be patient, gracious under fire, and able to direct the conversation back to explaining what makes the product a good one, how it can solve the customer's problems, and why they should buy it.

I often see successful SEs lean heavily on either their good technical skills or their interpersonal skills—or a blend of the two. In a technology context, it's a common line of demarcation; you're either good with people or you're good with tech. The two don't often mix. To succeed as a sales engineer, it's important to have a really good blend of both. In my experience, that's rare, and very valuable.

This role calls for less chest-thumping, less bravado, less charisma than, say, an outside salesperson. It's more factual. But it's still very much about selling, and something that many engineers can't naturally do. Sometimes engineers are too candid. I sometimes joke that you never want an engineer in the room with the customer, because they'll tell the truth. An engineer would say, "Our software is pretty buggy." A *sales* engineer would say, "This product is well-suited for early adopters." The difference is in the framing.

PROFILE

Greg Crist

Greg Crist, Sales Engineer, SPSS

In my almost thirty-year career, I spent ten years in small to medium-sized companies (one hundred to fifteen hundred employees). I then worked for ten years in very small, VC-funded startup companies. For the last ten years, I have worked for a startup that was acquired by IBM.

I was primarily drawn to the startup environment by my curiosity of the process and work required to build a company from nothing but an idea. I was drawn to startups because of my desire to learn about all aspects of the business. I wanted to learn and experience the building of a business from day one. The chance to build something from the ground up and have the chance to shape the product/service and the company was something I wanted to be a part of. The chance to work in an environment where the only limits were your imagination and to build a team to try and fulfill the business goal was also a strong draw for me.

Secondly, I wanted to have the freedom to choose how I performed my job and be measured on my actual results. I was never good at self-promotion, and I think a startup is good for people who want to be judged on their contributions without having to ask for it or sell it. I have heard many people say, "There is no place to hide in a startup. You either contribute or leave."

In the startup world, you get a lot of freedom to define your roles, responsibilities, and job title. You can have a direct conversation with anyone else in the company—whether that is the person who wrote the code or the HR representative about your health benefits. You work independently and manage your own priorities to a greater degree than in a larger corporation. The startup environment has less overhead, less overlay personnel who question your choices or try to define your priorities for you.

On the negative side, you are generally selling a product/solution for a market that has not been established, and your company's corporate name is not established, so it can be a challenge to convince people of the value of your solution. It can be a challenge to just get in the door. There is always more work to be done than there is time in the day. If you are not good at prioritizing and making decisions quickly without all the data, you will not be successful. You must be competent in performing your job or you will very quickly be pushed aside or out.

In a larger corporation, you spend the majority of your time (more than I think is useful) networking and communicating internally. To be successful in a larger corporation, you must build a brand for yourself and communicate your successes to the broader teams.

In a startup, you should spend the majority of your time networking and interacting with people *outside* of your company. You work more independently and need to evangelize your company/product and be learning and adjusting from what you pick up in the marketplace. Also, you don't have a brand identity like IBM that will get people to return your phone calls or emails.

Someone in a startup must be self-motivated and be comfortable working with minimal guidance. They must be self-reliant and willing to pitch in wherever necessary. It may be as simple as going out and buying dinner for the operations team as they launch a new service. It could be positioning the product to a new market or new business problem. You must take that vision and build out the story and sales materials without any help or any prior experience doing it.

Sales Operations

While speaking at an event once, I met a young woman from a large technology company who was thinking of moving into StartUpLand. She wanted to know whether her skills would be valued in a smaller company. I asked her what role she was currently playing. She replied, "Sales operations."

"Holy crap!" I said. "You'll be the most valuable hire a growth-stage company could ever make." Some people around us looked puzzled, and I realized that not everyone appreciates that Sales Operations (Sales Ops) is the secret weapon to scaling startups.

One of the largest friction points in rapid scaling is the sales force. Very few companies have a business model that enables frictionless revenue growth by way of the successful implementation of a freemium model (e.g., BetterCloud, Cloudflare, Dropbox, MongoDB), and even those that do eventually hire a sales team to move up the ladder on deal size and improve upsell, cross-sell, and renewal rates. When a startup begins to scale a sales force, it desperately needs to create a sales ops function. Here's why:

- The company needs to hire, train, and make productive a lot of new salespeople—fast. The sales directors and VPs will find it hard to take the time to sit with internal and external recruiters to write job descriptions, screen candidates, and develop the systematic training and monitoring and coaching programs for new sales recruits. The difference between on-ramping a productive salesperson in three months versus six months could be life or death for a scaling startup. That's the role of Sales Ops.

- The VP of Sales may be a great leader, but not a great operator. Most VPs of Sales are strong leaders of people, recruiters, and individual rainmakers, but they don't typically love staring at spreadsheets, analyzing metrics, and working out optimal compensation systems that align incentives with strategy. That's the role of Sales Ops.

- Sales and Marketing alignment is important, but hard to execute in the trenches. The sales directors and VPs are too busy chasing deals and coaching their reps in the field to be back in headquarters walking Marketing through the latest in competitive intelligence. The field staff struggles to be patient enough to explain and identify what sales tools are lacking as well as tracking what happened to certain cohorts of leads to improve lead generation. And wrangling over the latest in pricing and packaging schemes is never fun—and definitely not something a company will want a sales team distracted by. That's the role of Sales Ops.

- The insights from a sales customer relationship management (CRM) system are strategic, but cumbersome. A startup needs to have an in-house whiz at each of the various sales systems—like Salesforce.com, SugarCRM and NetSuite—to develop those fancy pipeline reports, prepare for the weekly sales calls, and report a snapshot of what is happening in the field across all territories and all sales teams to the executive team and the board on a weekly, monthly, and quarterly basis. That's the role of Sales Ops.

- To make Sales efficient, a startup needs to invest in technologies that facilitate efficiency without slowing sales down during its implementation. Sales organizations are full of technology that need to be mastered—the CRM, the dialer, the email platform, the analytics tools—thus asking each sales rep to develop proficiency in each tool and provide the IT team with feedback on how to optimally configure each tool is a distraction for them. That's the role of Sales Ops.

The best sales operations leaders allow the sales team to spend more time selling and less time worrying about reporting, cross-functional coordination, and operational management. The sales ops person's role is akin to serving as the chief of staff to the Chief Revenue Officer and is the absolute secret weapon that every company needs to rapidly scale sales.

Sales Operations generally starts up once a company has perhaps ten to fifteen salespeople—when it gets past the point at which an individual can manage all of them effectively and starts to need layers of management. With those layers comes the need for operational support. By this point, a company might have some established processes, but it has become time to invest in maturing those processes.

The thing about Sales Ops is *you're not selling*. You don't have to be the car salesman. You don't have to travel. You don't necessarily need a sales background to undertake the role. In many ways, Sales Ops is the product manager of the sales organization. As a former product manager, that may be one of the reason I am drawn to the position—it's so central and important.

Every time I walk into a board meeting at one of my portfolio companies, for example, I want to know if my stock price is going up or down—the value of my equity. I want to know if the company is on plan to hit its revenue targets or off-plan and why. I want to know the growth trajectory, and what the company's going to look like next year.

All of that falls on the CEO, who turns to the VP of Sales, who (often behind the scenes) turns to the Director of Sales Operations and says, *What do you think we can do next year? How are we doing this quarter? Are we going to hit our number or not? How does it feel?* This information then goes back up to the CEO and board, who set the public's expectations.

So the Director of Sales Ops has to be very precise in gathering information from sales reps and making sure that the forecasts are accurate. Little mistakes have big ripple effects. In a startup, maybe you run out of cash or you don't get funded the next year because you don't make your numbers. You are at the *hub* of the revenue-generating machine for the company. Your actions have enormous effect and influence on revenue generation. So stakes are very high, and your impact is very high.

As a sales ops leader, organization is key, as is the need for precision. You're the person, after all, who will be focused on making the team more efficient and effective. You'll be putting all your analytical chops to work to help make the company a selling powerhouse. You also need to be a good administrator and very analytical, as you'll often be calculating quotas and compensation formulas (the most important thing for a sales rep).

Finally, it's important to be a good communicator and negotiator, because you'll be negotiating with the reps all the time. The reps don't report to Sales Ops, but Sales Ops does need to direct the reps. You negotiate compensation plans with the sales reps, and you negotiate forecasts, and you try to direct them appropriately. You have to decide whether you push the reps harder or go easy, whether to hold them accountable with the stick or to dangle the carrot. This is the job of the VP of Sales, yes, but the Director of Sales Operations often gets involved as well. You have to love maximizing effectiveness; you have to love that dynamic. If you get a jolt of energy from seeing things work more efficiently and coaching people and setting up organizational models, then Sales Ops is a great fit for you.

To use a theater analogy, Sales Operations is the stage manager—the person who directs the lighting, sound system, the set design, the rehearsal schedule. You're not onstage—you're supporting the people onstage. You're helping making it all work well.

It's an exciting role because you get to work with all these fantastic, charismatic, entertaining people who have a huge impact on the business without the burden of *being* that person.

Account Management

More and more, account managers are becoming a valued part of any startup's sales team, particularly in light of the popular trend of the SaaS-based business model. SaaS translates to "software as a service," and it depends heavily on renewals.

The whole economic model is this: If a startup is going to deliver software as a service to its customers, it wants the customer to keep using that service continuously for the next six years, not to cancel after six months. Acquiring new customers is expensive; on the other hand, long-standing customers who renew year in and year out are very profitable. Thus, the lifeblood of scaling startups is customer retention.

The job of the sales rep is to make the sale and move on to the next customer. The job of the account manager is to work with the acquired customers—to support them, to manage implementation, to deal with any questions they have or issues that come up now or long into the future, and most importantly, to ensure renewal and avoid having customers churn out. It's a critical role regarding keeping customers happy and maintaining renewal rates.

Usually, there's an account management team or a couple of account managers who are joined at the hip with the salespeople and who report in to the head of Sales or the Chief Revenue Officer.

Consider the idea of hunters and gatherers. The salespeople are the hunters—they hunt, they kill the prey, and they bring the prey back to the camp. The gatherers, meanwhile, handle the skinning, cook the meat, and gather the fruits from the harvest to complete the meal. This is the account manager. In this role, you focus on taking advantage of the success of the salespeople who have already secured the contracts and making sure that the accounts stay successful. As soon as a startup in an enterprise B2B situation makes it to ten or twenty customers, it's time to get an account management team.

Salespeople get paid to hunt. They don't focus on the long-term success of accounts. If they spent all their time hand-holding customers, they would have no time to go out to get the next sale, to hit the next quarter's numbers. The salespeople should be pushing the frontier, moving forward, acquiring new customers. The account management team should be back at home nurturing, supporting the existing customers, helping them be successful, and then ensuring renewal and perhaps even expansion.

None of this is to say the account management job lacks exciting moments. I've seen situations in which an account manager was in a position to make or break the startup by dealing with a client at a pivotal moment. One company I know of provided augmented services for airlines and banks and other enterprise clients. At one point, a particular bank was the startup's most important customer in terms of revenue, and the bank was unhappy. After the financial crisis, the bank had come under a lot of regulatory scrutiny, and the people there were very sensitive to the accuracy of the dollars and credit flowing through it, and the reporting of all of that, and they felt that this startup wasn't accurate enough. The startup, which was young at the time, was really buttoned-down, but not as buttoned-down as the bank needed it to be. So when the bank expressed its unhappiness and threatened to cancel the relationship, the startup had to scramble to make things right. The bank represented probably 25–30 percent of the startup's revenue at that point, so losing it as a customer would have been the death of the company. It would have run out of money, and been unable to raise more. And so it scrambled to ensure that it served the bank's needs and solved all of the bank's compliance problems.

This was all very frustrating, because none of this generated any more income or business for the startup. But the bank had a compliance issue, and that's black and white. The bank had regulators breathing down its neck and its staff was facing a lot of pressure from senior management. They had a problem, and the startup had to solve that problem. That's what an account management person does.

And I think that's why working in Account Management has a big draw. You get to solve problems. You get to help people. It's a really important function for the company, and it makes the business work. Without it, the business can fail.

From a practical standpoint, it also involves less travel than some other sales positions, so it's a steadier job with fewer peaks and valleys, although being close to customers is critical and sometimes you can only do this by periodically visiting them and building that relationship. If you're more suited to that kind of environment, Account Management might be the right fit for you.

PROFILE

Tracy Cronlund

Tracy Cronlund, Vice President of Global Account Sales, Tracx

> Our sales team is broken into four groups: Business Development/Lead Generation (aka inside sales), Mid-Market (new sales), Enterprise (new sales), and Account Executives (my team, account sales). The business development team works to get leads and meetings set for the sales teams that are trying to bring in new clients (mid-market and enterprise teams). Once the client signs up on an annual contract, my team takes over. We assign a business account manager to a specific account for the duration of their contract, with the main goal being to help the client see

value and benefit all year, so that they ultimately renew and buy more product. My team aren't "trainers," but we work closely with the services and support teams to make sure the clients are comfortable in the system and that their how-to and technical questions are answered in a timely manner.

Today, I manage a team of four people and also run the department, which means I have a hand in the decision-making processes that will affect the future of this group and the company. In a previous similar position at a larger organization, I managed a team of twelve account salespeople and was not involved in any larger decision-making processes within the company. There are many differences from that role, which I have included below.

My specific responsibilities include:

- Working with my team members individually on deal setup, technical product resolutions, forecasting, negotiating tactics, escalation needs, demo prep work, and other coaching/learning/problem-solving opportunities.

- Traveling to visit clients onsite for meetings. I often go around the country, and sometimes abroad, to meet personally with some accounts on the state of their business with us, renewal and new product opportunities, and product enhancement requests.

- Tracking client behavior. I keep an extremely organized collection of our current client base, including renewal amounts, products subscribed to, dates of expirations, etc.

- Working on larger and complex renewals. With a small team and client base, I am more personally involved in some sales cycles than I would be with a bigger team.

- Working and meeting with other departments within the company. I am often in meetings with the product or services leadership teams to talk about product roadmap items, technical requests, and best practice requests from clients. I represent the voice of the customer in internal meetings to make sure their needs are being met today and going forward.

- Working and meeting with senior leadership to help build the Account Sales department. Since we are still a young company, much decision-making power has been given to me, and I often get involved in decisions that will shape not only my team, but also the future team members and eventually different teams and managers that will come later as we grow as a company. For example, we had to work on creating compensation plans, goals for the team, bookings policies, setup of internal systems, and a variety of different daily processes that have become routine for the reps. Being part of a smaller startup company gave me the opportunity to help with this ground-up process, whereas in a previous role at a larger and more established organization, these things were decided long before I was there, and when there were organizational changes, since there were so many other managers in my exact same role, my voice wouldn't often be heard or have as much of an impact as it does today.

I am drawn to smaller companies and startups and prefer to work at them. Some of the reasons for this I have listed above. But also I like the unknown/uncertainty/excitement that comes with the "Will we succeed?" factor. I have always been competitive, and working at a startup feels a little like that. Of course you have your day-to-day work (as with any company) but behind that (as you are usually reminded of at the end of every quarter) is that feeling of "How are we doing?" and "Will this work?" which makes my overall work life more fulfilling and interesting. Of course I also like the financial carrot that is usually dangling for most employees of startups, with some stock options. I am now financially as well as emotionally invested. Which makes that possibility of "Will we succeed?" and "How big will we get?" that much more exciting.

Client Services

Sometimes, the labels blur. That is, there's often no distinction between Account Management and Client Services. Other times, Account Management is more selling oriented and Client Services is more service oriented, which is to say, the client services function involves assisting with customer needs in the moment. The client services team is often reacting to complaints or problems that arise as customers use the product. These questions may, for example, address things like, *I have identified a few bugs that need fixing. I'm struggling with implementation or integration. The most recent version that you shipped out is incompatible with my data.*

If the salespeople are the hunters, Account Management and Client Services are both very much the gatherers. They both focus on long-term customer retention.

Client Services is more of a good Samaritan, charitable function. They're empathetic and react to other people's problems when they arise, whereas Account Management tends to be more proactive and a bit more strategic in anticipating potential issues.

Even so, sometimes the best customer service or client service organizations are actually effective *sales* organizations. You've probably experienced this when talking on the phone with a service provider: *Is there anything else I can help you with? By the way, I noticed on your account that you're using up your data plan every month. I have a special data plan upgrade program that I could put you into that will save you money.* That's what a client services person does.

Essentially, they might sound and act like tech support, but they're selling. The best-trained client services organizations are effective at selling, upselling, and cross-selling.

Upselling is encouraging customers to buy more of the same thing. Using Dropbox as an example again, when upselling, you might suggest buying more gigabytes of storage; that is, using the same product even more, resulting in a higher annual fee and thus more revenue for the company. Cross-selling, on the other hand, involves suggesting, *Now that you're using this thing, why don't you also buy this other thing?* A classic cross-sell might be something like saying, *You bought a pair of pants. Do you want a belt with that? Do you want a pair of socks with that?*

In Client Services, you're in the service business. You wake up every day and say, *How can I help you? How can I make your life easier? How can I help you achieve your goals?*

You also need to be organized—and strategic in your thinking about the goals of the company. You're always thinking about what the company is trying to achieve, how it gets more revenue right now and over time. The rewarding part is that you're doing this in a positive way—a way that's good for the customer and authentic.

In addition to empathy, intuition is a helpful quality for this role. Customers may not come out and say what they need. The worst situation you can be in is when a customer cancels and you don't know why. Even worse, you're *surprised*. A customer cancels, and you say, *What? They canceled? Why did they cancel? I don't know. I'm shocked, I thought they were happy*. But maybe you didn't really know if they were happy or not.

A client services person needs to know. It's about knowing what's going on with customers. If they're using the product. If the product is meeting their needs. If they're happy with the product. If they have the support of the rest of the organization. These are key things in customer happiness. So you need to be a good listener, connect with customers and treat them like partners, and work toward really understanding their needs.

A popular label in startups for the client services function is *customer success*. Some startups hire an individual head of customer success, the Customer Success Manager, to report in to the head of client services and be empowered to be the customer's advocate within the organization. Other times, that function might be elevated. However the role is defined, it serves a similar function: to galvanize the organization to make customers happy, successful, and retained.

Professional Services

For a period of time, I ran Professional Services at my startup, Open Market. We were selling e-commerce software, helping businesses get online so they could sell their products and services securely. This time period, the mid-1990s, was the Internet 1.0 days. It was often the first time the companies we worked with had ever gone online. We helped them with shopping carts, secure payments, content management, and catalogs.

We had gone from zero to building this incredibly complex system in a year, which was no small feat, but our selling and value proposition evolved quickly as we and the market matured.

At first, we said, *Here's a secure but somewhat raw payment platform. Now go figure it out.* Customers would then immediately wonder how to integrate the product into their environment. They'd wonder how to build their websites, how to build their content and catalogs, and how to fit our product into their payment infrastructures. We were selling hammers to carpenters (metaphorically speaking), and the carpenters were willing to take the tool we had and figure out how to put it to use.

But carpenters, as you might guess, need, let's say, twenty-seven different kinds of tools. A hammer alone is not enough. We needed to move more into *solutions*, where we could offer them a complete "carpentry set" designed just for them.

So that's what we did. We shifted toward saying, *We'll build your catalog and teach you how to build a better e-commerce site. We'll integrate it with your ERP systems. We'll integrate it with your payment system. We'll do the whole thing. And oh yeah, two or three of our products come with that, and you'll pay for that, but you're also going to pay for us to integrate and deliver the whole solution.* That is what Professional Services does.

In the early days of a B2B startup (this doesn't so much apply in B2C situations, where there is zero customization per user), a startup's pitch goes like this: *Here's what our product does, here are the features, here is the functionality, here are its benefits, and here's why you should buy it.* That is, the company's job is to figure out how the product solves the customer's problem.

As a market matures, and as a startup matures, it shifts toward selling solutions. This means solving the problem *for* the customer. The product is now part of a toolkit; the thing being sold is now a solution to a problem rather than an individual product.

As companies mature, they deliver a broader sales process and sales-delivery capability, which is what the customers demand in more established markets. The professional services organization implements the product and then fits it, and other things around your product, into a customer's environment to solve a problem in a more complete way. It's kind of like the difference between going to a store to buy your own clothes and enlisting a personal shopper. On your own, you have to figure out how the clothes at a store combine to solve your fashion needs. With a personal shopper, someone works to put together a few outfits and solve it *for* you.

Professional services teams within a company are like mini consulting firms centered around their product. By way of comparison, Accenture and IBM Services are examples of big consulting firms. Over the last ten years, IBM has shifted from being a software products company to being a services and solutions company. They go to a big retailer and say, *We're going to set you up to be an e-commerce juggernaut. You'll use three or four of our products and two of our partners' products as part of your solution, and we'll stitch them all together and integrate it all into your environment and customize it to be just right for you.*

Sometimes, Professional Services even involves offering custom development, such as customizing the product to integrate with the customer's other products. When we first started shipping our product at Open Market, a lot of our customers said they needed this feature or that feature to work a little differently. When a customer asks for that, a startup has two options. One option is you go to the engineering team and say, *Drop everything. I know you're working on the next great feature that's outlined in the product roadmap, the next product release, but I need you to solve this customer's problem and have that feature work differently for them.*

That's a bad approach for obvious reasons, but sometimes you don't have a choice if the customer represents a big portion of your business. You put the product roadmap on the shelf and redirect your resources to solve the customer's problem.

The second option is the one I see more frequently and, if you can pull it off, is better for the startup. You say, *Let's get a professional services person in here who knows our product intimately, who knows how to work with the configuration, and who knows how to write to the APIs* [application programming interfaces], *and let's have them customize that feature.* The big rule if you're pursuing this option, which I share with my students and startups alike: *Never, ever fork the code* (split the product into multiple versions, each of which does something slightly different and requires its own maintenance and development). This approach allows you to abstract portions of the product in such a way that enables it to be customized via an API so you solve the problem of the customer without ever touching the engineering organization or disturbing the product roadmap.

Companies have to build up professional services teams to do that kind of custom development—to protect the product team and to solve customer problems at the same time.

In an e-commerce setting, for example, you might have a customer who wants the user interface to look a certain way, who wants the catalog to be presented differently than it is by default. The customer may even want custom task flow based on the ways its own customers enter the site—for example, responding to a mobile ad versus a search ad, or accessing the website directly. Your customer may also already have an order management system and inventory system, a payment system, and so on, and want to have all of that integrated into its e-commerce system. Doing this would require custom integration and custom development.

In doing this, good professional services teams then become an asset to the company, because Sales can now say, *Not only does our product have all these fantastic features, we also have this great service organization that can customize it and integrate it into your particular environment.*

Notice the theme here? Delivering highly customized solutions that are right for the customer in their environment that meets their needs—that's the job of the professional services team.

Installation and Training

Let's say your company decides to buy software from Salesforce .com to try to make the sales team more efficient and transparent. Okay, great. What happens next? How do you actually *use* the product? How do you load up your data?

Companies need to be able to use the software they buy effectively. This means making sure staff is trained on that software and knows how to use it. In this case, every Salesforce.com sales rep needs to know how to use the product—how to enter records, handle issues, and all sorts of other things. Salesforce.com, then, might have trainers who go into those companies. Those people would be from the professional services team (in some cases, they're part of a separate organization reporting to Sales).

When a startup's customers need *help* using the product—installing it, integrating it, getting its staff trained on its usage—the installation and training team are the people who handle these services. They can also help a customer get the product up and running and loaded up with the customer's data.

Each of these functions can be a great entry point for people new to a startup because professional services people are on the front lines, working with customers. They get to know the product. They get to know the customer needs. They're very boots-on-the-ground and pragmatic. They're in the field, seeing the environment. This enables them to become incredibly familiar with the product and its customers, which can translate to being able to move into other roles.

Good professional services people, for example, sometimes become product managers, sales engineers, and even software developers. This is because the really good professional services people are very technical. They help integrate the product with the customer environment and in writing connecting code and custom scripts and things of that nature. Over time, they can learn to become software developers and become part of the product team.

As discussed previously, in the world of startups, you have a lot more fluidity as to which roles you take on. It's one of the things that's so great about building a career in StartUpLand; you don't have to stay stuck in a silo. You can move from one role to the next over the course of three, four, five, six years. That kind of flexibility and mobility is far less common in larger companies.

How Context Shapes the Sales Organization

As with other startup functions, the sales organization evolves as the startup matures. Both the development stage of the company and the nature of and relationship to the customer influence these changes.

Context: Stage

In other chapters, I've talked about the different phases of a startup's life cycle. In each phase, the roles look different. For Sales, in the jungle phase, you are mostly doing expeditionary and evangelical sales—you are breaking new ground and trying to sort out the sales formula. In the dirt-road phase, you look more for repeatability, and you begin to find your groove and develop processes. In the highway phase, you get to optimize and scale; it's time to build up the machine. Hence, what a sales role looks like changes over time. In the early days, you're more like a product manager who happens to sell; later, you're a salesperson who happens to provide product feedback. It's a very different dynamic.

If you're somebody who enjoys the figuring-it-out stage, then you want to be in Sales in the earliest phases of a company's development. If you don't like figuring it out—if you'd like things to be figured out *for* you, and to just do the work—then you want to be in the later stages of the sales organization.

This isn't to say that in Sales, your job becomes more or less interesting depending on where you're at in the stage of the startup. It just means that scaling challenges evolve over time, and that different stages of a startup's evolution may fit better for different people.

Let's imagine an SaaS startup. At first, the founders do the selling; one of the cofounders leads the sales efforts personally. This is very early in the sales learning curve. They're trying to learn how to sell, and even how to describe the product in the first place. They're learning what their buyers need and what their environment looks like. They're in an exploratory phase.

Over time, they hire a few salespeople—often initially an outside salesperson and maybe an inside salesperson, depending on the business model and how expensive the product is. The cofounder tries to transfer what she's learned to the salesperson, and then let those first salespeople loose to see if they can close some sales and achieve an initial quota.

Once the founders feel like that salesperson is becoming successful, they might hire another salesperson. Then another. And another. If sales keep moving, the founders generally relinquish personal control over the organization and hire a head of Sales. Over time, they'll initially build out a small sales organization and then a larger one as the company grows.

Companies tend to add salespeople at the point when they think those added salespeople can be productive. Salespeople are very expensive, and when a startup invests in them, they start paying their salaries immediately, but the salespeople need to be trained over a three- or six-month period before becoming productive.

In other words, companies go into a cash hole whenever they hire a new salesperson.

Recognizing this initial cost, the startup has to evaluate whether it can justify the investment of a new salesperson each time they hire one. Will that person pay back in six months? In nine months? In twelve months? Can the company afford that delay?

When a startup decides to ramp sales, the other dimension it needs to consider is how many leads it has. Sometimes you want to invest more in marketing to generate more leads to make the existing sales team more productive as opposed to hiring more salespeople who are going to spread the leads too thinly across the team.

What does this all mean to you?

It means you want to be savvy about evaluating and understanding what stage a startup is in when you are considering joining it. One important indicator is how many sales reps the startup has, what the total quota is that the aggregate group of salespeople is targeting, and how rapidly the sales organization has grown. These are all good signals for what stage the company is in and how successful it is at the time. So if you like the jungle phase, look for companies with very few salespeople. If you like the highway phase, look for an established team with a head of Sales and steadily growing sales numbers and quotas.

And go ahead and ask some tough questions. Ask, *What was the sales quota attainment last year?* If a company has added too much sales capacity too quickly ahead of its ability to make those sales people productive, its quota attainment is going to be at a low percentage—maybe 60 or 70 percent. Those are bad numbers. But if the startup is hiring in a measured fashion and is seeing aggregate quota attainment of 85 for 90 or 100 percent, those are really good numbers. Over 100 percent, of course, is fantastic. It means the company desperately needs more sales reps and, arguably has underhired.

Another question to ask is about the team's win/loss rate; you can use the answer to develop your own judgment as to what it might look like for you going forward in the sales role. Every salesperson competing for deals has a win/loss rate; that is, what percentage of the deals a company is winning versus losing to the competition. If the win/loss rate is 70 or 80 percent, that is a great number. If the win/loss rate is 20 or 25 percent, that is a bad number. It means the company is investing time and energy into getting to the table and doing demos and filling out RFPs and answering questions, and yet it's only converting one out of four of those situations into an actual revenue-generating event.

As an individual coming into a sales organization, you want to know that people are successful. You want to know that sales reps are hitting their numbers.

Context: Customer Type

The other element of context that is important to consider with the sales function is who is the target customer, the average contract value for the customer, and therefore what is the sales model that has been constructed to go after that customer. In this chapter, I have discussed the different kinds of sales personnel and models—field sales, inside sales, self-service sales. Table 6-1 summarizes these different models by customer type: consumer/prosumer (either a consumer or an individual professional), small or mid-sized business (SMB), or large enterprise. For each customer type, I frame what the typical average contract value (ACV) might be for the product. The ACV is an important barometer for the type of sales model: low ACV business models can't afford to have anything

TABLE 6-1

Sales models by customer type

Customer	ACV	Sales model
Consumer/prosumer	<$1,000	Self-service
SMB	$1,000–$10,000	Inside sales
Mid-market	$10,000–$100,000	Field sales + inside sales
Enterprise	>$100,000	Field sales

other than self-service whereas high ACV business models can afford a large field sales and support team.

Attributes of a Salesperson

The qualities of a great salesperson depend on the type of sales the person is handling. I've touched on those qualities while discussing each different kind of role, but to add a few more, I think that having high emotional and social intelligence is critical. Being able to read people, to empathize with them, and navigate situations—these are all huge positive requirements and attributes of effective salespeople.

Tracy Cronlund, the account management VP featured earlier in this chapter, offers a few additional attributes:

> *Independence/ability to think on your feet.* There are usually fewer resources at smaller companies, so you have to learn how to do things on your own and have some independence, rather than always asking for direction or having someone telling you what to do. For example, we don't have a formal onboarding program for new employees just yet. When someone starts, their manager sets them up with a few sessions with other employees and then essentially that new employee is on their own to work with their colleagues and seek out the resources needed to do their job. The employee owns the process, which can be great for some, but others might feel uncomfortable. At a larger organization I was once part of, I went through a very carefully organized and scheduled six-week training program. There were many classes and tests, and every minute was accounted for. I didn't have any control over my program nor any ability to change or modify it. But on a positive note, it felt "safe" knowing that everything was done for me, and all I needed to do was show up and pay attention.

Competitiveness/confidence. I think you need to feel some competitiveness to work at a startup. Maybe that is just in the sales role, but maybe in any role within the whole organization, not just within your internal team. There is definitely the sense of "Will this succeed?" and "Can we perform better than a competitor or similar company?" that seems to be always present in the back of my mind at a smaller company starting out. I think you have to feel comfortable with the idea of risk and have confidence that where you are and what you are doing is the best it can be, so that you and the company can succeed.

Not afraid of change. Obviously, with a small company there will be lots of change in processes, product, tools, and maybe even leadership, office locations, and day-to-day responsibilities. I am not only comfortable with all of this, I embrace and look forward to trying new things and am very open to my day-to-day changing and evolving.

Want to work as part of a team. With a smaller company you are drawn closer to your immediate colleagues and sometimes to everyone in the whole company. I myself am an extrovert and thrive in this kind of workspace, but can see how others may want to keep to themselves, do their work, collect their paycheck, and go home at night.

Not afraid to have work become a bigger part of your life. "Work hard, play hard" really does ring true with some of the smaller companies I have worked for. I work all hours and all days of the week, and so does my team. I feel so much like I am contributing to something bigger and I enjoy the work, I don't mind. This is not a 9–5 job. There is less structure and an informal work hour schedule. People appreciate those who need to rush home to be with their families every night. I have been lucky enough to work at startups where the senior leaders felt comfortable letting their employees have more flex time and vacation time, since we were working so many long hours.

As Cronlund observes, the sales function in StartUpLand is definitely not a 9–5 job. The stakes are too high, month after month, quarter after quarter, year after year. There's a funny habit that all my startups have. Every six months, they come to me and say, "These coming six months are the most important ever in the company's history." And they're right. The next six months are always the most important. And Sales is at the heart of that.

RESOURCES

For more about sales roles and skills in StartUpLand, I recommend:

Books

- Roberge, Mark. *The Sales Acceleration Formula* (New York: Wiley & Sons, 2015). Roberge was VP of Sales at Hubspot and shares his playbook for data-driven, inbound, and outbound selling.

- Ross, Aaron and Marylou Tyler. *Predictable Revenue* (2011). This book provides the definitive treatise on how to build a demand-generation and sales machine that is scalable and repeatable.

Articles

- Leslie, Mark and Halloway, Charles. "The Sales Learning Curve." *Harvard Business Review*, July–August 2006. This *Harvard Business Review* article is the bible for startup founders and sales executives to help think through the right sales approach for the various startup stages.

7. **Finance**

There is a funny ritual that happens in board rooms when it comes time to determining which board members will sit on which board committees. I have seen the same scenario play out on almost every board on which I have ever served.

"OK," starts the CEO hesitantly. "It's time to select committees. Who wants to be on audit?" Smirks and eye rolls ensue. Everyone knows the audit committee is a snoozefest, and finance has a reputation for being the last place you want to spend your time as a board member, particularly when compared with the thrill of developing innovative products or the adrenaline involved with sales.

At least that is the conventional wisdom. Trust me when I tell you that an effective and powerful finance function is critical to the success of startups.

Like Marketing, many startups wait until it's too late to staff the finance function. And when they do, they often under-resource it. They bring in a bookkeeper or outsource the function to a local consulting shop and suddenly realize they're scrambling to catch up with the demands of the role.

I had that happen once, and I lost a lot of money because of it. One of my portfolio companies was scaling fast—really fast. We had tripled in revenue and Marketing was reporting that they could grow even faster if we just gave them more budget to spend on customer acquisition. With all that growth, we found ourselves in the awkward position of having a Finance and

Operations department run by a junior bookkeeper. Our CEO was so busy driving growth, he was slow to bring a strong VP of Finance on board. The executive we finally hired quickly dug in to the financials and the cash flow and came to the first board meeting ashen-faced. She had discovered that we had inaccurately accounted for many of our transactions. A company we thought was profitable was in fact still generating losses, and our accelerated customer acquisition had only dug a larger hole for ourselves. We slammed on the brakes, but it was too late. A company we thought would generate a huge win ended up resulting in a total loss of all our money.

So, believe me when I say that the finance function is a critically important one in startups, and working in a startup finance department can be incredibly challenging, exciting, and rewarding.

The finance function at a startup is typically responsible for many activities, including planning, modeling, closing the books, running the audit, reporting the numbers, managing the cash flow, handling billing, and collecting receivables as well as processing payables. Often, the finance function is also in charge of a lot of the administrative areas, such as HR, IT, legal, investor relations, facilities management (i.e., space planning, managing the physical office, negotiating, and securing leases), and some of the nuts-and-bolts operational stuff that needs to be taken off the shoulders of the entrepreneurs and the engineers.

When the finance function works really well, it acts as a business partner to the CEO. Finance will help identify the appropriate investments required to grow the business, raise the necessary capital for business expansion, forge strategic partnerships, and help create cross-functional efficiency throughout the organization to ensure the company can scale up and, ultimately, become profitable. The finance function is like the lubricant in a car; it makes the engine perform more smoothly and allows all the parts to work more effectively. Also like car lubricant, however, it is easy to forget to maintain the right levels—and when you neglect it, major problems can result.

Finance Roles

The finance function for startups has four primary areas of focus:

- Controller

- Financial planning and analysis (FP&A)

- Business operations

- Fundraising and investor relations

In the early stages of most startups (i.e., the jungle phase), one or two individuals might be hired to perform the tactical activities required for the finance function to operate. Outsourced firms are popular in the early stages as well, either to perform the actual day-to-day tasks or, more often, to provide part-time strategic oversight to the more junior, full-time staff members. As a startup grows into the dirt-road phase and gets to, say thirty to fifty employees, it will often hire a more senior executive to serve as the director or VP of Finance to oversee a small finance department. Eventually, at two hundred to three hundred employees, there might be a Chief Financial Officer (CFO) supervising individual directors or vice presidents who have the appropriate specialized skills and experience to serve in each of the four areas described below.

Controller

In the earliest days of a startup, when you are under ten employees, there is often no revenue and modest expenses, typically tied to payroll. Thus, the accounting activities are simple enough to outsource to a bookkeeper who manages day-to-day transactions, pays the bills and makes sure the payroll is processed.

As a company grows and begins to bring in its first revenue, as well as raises funds from outside investors, a controller is hired to lead all the accounting activities. Put simply, the controller is the "bean counter" in the company. In terms of background, controllers will typically be certified public accountants (CPAs) and often have begun their careers at one of the large accounting and auditing firms, such as Deloitte, PwC, Ernst & Young, or KPMG.

To be an effective controller, there are several things to focus on.

THE CONTROLLER'S MISSION: STAY IN CONTROL. The controller's job is focused on accuracy, precision, and implementing internal controls. The controller is responsible for designing and implementing the company's chart of accounts and general ledger. She records the revenue transactions in accordance with established revenue recognition policies, pays the company's bills, and records its accounts payable and accounts receivable. The controller prepares the company's financial statements, including the income statement, the cash flow statement, and the balance sheet. She designs and executes the processes used to close the company books each month, quarter, and year-end.

AUDITS ARE GOOD FOR YOU, HONEST. The controller is also responsible for managing the company's annual audit, something that is not typically done in the first few years of a startup's existence but often attended to in the third or fourth year, when a few rounds of financing have been completed and revenue is beginning to be earned. As part of managing the audit process, the controller will select and oversee the work of an outside accounting firm to prepare the company's audited financials each year. The controller works with the auditors to review customer and vendor agreements, assess the appropriateness of the company's revenue recognition policies, test that the appropriate procedures and governance policies are in place and being followed, and correct any errors or misrepresentations. Through the annual audit process and in general, the controller is constantly assessing and monitoring the company's controls and processes.

Speaking of the audit, as an investor, I am a big fan of audits and auditors. I know that may sound strange coming from someone who is an entrepreneur at heart. Rest assured, it's not because I'm a masochist. As a point of comparison, most of us are not fans of going to the dentist for our biannual checkups. But we are certainly happy when we can avoid dental problems that would arise due to lack of attention. Similarly, an audit is a very important and valuable function that ensures the company's financials are accurate and its internal controls are sound (I know my finance friends are going to give me a hard time for comparing audits with going to the dentist, but I'm willing to risk it to make the point).

In a startup, the controller is like a company's operations chief, tucked away behind the scenes in the finance department but connected to all operations within the company. Everything needs to run smoothly under the controller's watchful eye. The bills need to be paid on time, the cash must be collected and posted to the right customer invoice in a timely manner, employees must be compensated properly, taxes paid properly, and so forth.

The accuracy of the financial statements is a critical responsibility of controllers. They have to prepare those statements, ensuring revenue and expenses are recognized properly based on generally accepted accounting principles, or GAAP (a set of accounting standards that dictates how a company presents its financial statements so that when one company reports, say, "gross margins," the meaning of that figure is the same as for every other company). It is imperative that everything be properly and carefully documented to make it easy on the auditors when they review the company's accounting records on an annual basis to ensure everything is in order. The integrity of the company's accounting is essential to ensuring management has a good handle on the ongoing performance of the business and is also essential to provide current and prospective investors confidence in the health of the underlying business.

WORKING WITH OTHER FUNCTIONS. There is often a level of healthy tension between the controller and the other functions in the company, particularly Sales. When it comes to reviewing contracts and determining revenue recognition, the finance function—typically the controller—has the final say. They review the customer contracts line by line, often helping draft the agreements or coordinating the work with an outside law firm.

Think about the incentives involved in customer contracts. Salespeople care about closing the deal and earning their commissions. They are paid to close deals month in, month out. A startup depends on the controller to review the customer contracts carefully and maintain consistent terms and conditions. The controller will often develop contract policies in conjunction with the VP of Sales and CEO and then make sure each contract complies with those policies as well as the company's pricing and revenue recognition policies. But in the heat of battle, with the success of the quarter on the line, each salesperson is often primarily focused on satisfying the prospective customer's needs and closing the deal. These two, sometimes conflicting, goals can be a source of friction. But the friction can be healthy; it may cause certain contract issues to get escalated to the appropriate senior executives and provide insight into deeper business issues. For example, the pricing structure may be too inflexible and outdated relative to where the market and competition has evolved, or perhaps the inadequacies of the product are forcing salespeople to give away too much functionality for free. In any event, you can expect some good, healthy debates between Sales and Finance throughout the customer contract process.

Financial Planning and Analysis (FP&A)

Often, startups can initially only afford to have one senior finance person on staff. So that person is expected to handle a wide range of responsibilities. Given the importance of accurate accounting, the controller is more typically the first senior finance hire and will be asked to cover other aspects of the finance role. But as the startup grows and there are results and metrics worth analyzing, another function grows in importance, and a new leader is brought in separately to establish it: the head of Financial Planning and Analysis.

There are a few key elements to the FP&A role. The first, not altogether surprising because of its name, is planning.

STARTUP PLANNING. At the very earliest stage of a startup, the financial planning work falls to the founding entrepreneur or a cofounder with strong "spreadsheet" skills. Here's how it typically works. When a startup is first created, the entrepreneur has to determine what will be needed to fund the business. The business might be *bootstrapped* initially—funded with the founder's own money or through customer revenues generated by the fledgling business. So, the founder creates a rudimentary plan in a spreadsheet to estimate just how much capital will be needed to get the business off the ground. Often, however, outside investment is sought to fund the business. In this case, the founder has to "pitch" investors. To do so, she might create a financial model, which is typically a spreadsheet that contains the expected operating expenses (headcount, rent, systems costs, and everything else) and expected revenue over a period of time. The model shows investors what the company is going to do with all that money they are about to wire.

After reviewing thousands of financial models that have been presented to me as a venture capital investor, I can guarantee two things about the financial model created by the entrepreneur. First, it will be characterized as "conservative," even though at almost every startup I've ever been involved with, everything takes longer to happen, costs more, and ramps more slowly than the entrepreneur thinks it will. Second, the financial model will be wrong. Forecasting the future is an impossible task, particularly in the dynamic world of startups. Thus, the model will be wrong as soon as it's created.

THE ANALYSIS. After a startup gets going, the real numbers start to come to light and the startup refines its model. That's where the FP&A function comes in. The FP&A function is the individual or group of individuals that focus on the planning and budgeting, an important and very fluid function.

Every year, typically in December or January, a startup has to submit an annual budget for approval to its board of directors. The budget will often contain a detailed assessment of what has happened in the past and, based on a number of key assumptions, a model is developed for the upcoming year. In addition to next year's budget—often called the *plan of record*—there will be a forecast for the next two to three years so that the board has a sense for where things are heading in the future. Remember, startups often need an infusion of new cash every twelve to twenty-four months, so this budget is not only important for communicating the performance of the business to the board but also to prospective investors.

FP&A generally drives the planning process that goes into creating the budget. That planning process involves getting input from every department throughout the company (bottom-up) and blending it with the entrepreneur's view of what should actually happen (top-down). The CEO may declare that the company needs to grow revenue by 100 percent and then turn to Sales and demand that it sign up for the increased number. Sales then turns to Marketing and Product to ask for more leads and product enhancements. Product turns to Engineering to ask for more resources to have the capacity to deliver the features. And around we go. FP&A has to drive that process, reconcile it, roll it up, lead the debate and discussion among the executive team, and eventually smooth it all out so that a budget is created where all departments are bought in and aligned. In well-run startups, that process will begin in the fall and continue for many months.

Toward the end of the planning process, the FP&A folks will run sensitivity analyses against the key assumptions. These "what if" scenarios, based on certain key variables, provide management with insights as to what model factors are most impactful. For example, the model assumes the sales team will achieve 90 percent of its quota of $1.5 million per sales rep, but what if it only achieves 75 percent? We assume gross margins will improve from 75 percent to 80 percent because of the following scale efficiencies that we expect, but what if we're wrong and they stay at 75 percent? We assume we can move days sales outstanding (i.e., how quickly the company collects cash from sales) from seventy-five to sixty days, but what if we're wrong and it stays at seventy-five days? These are the kinds of sensitivity questions the FP&A department will run through with the CEO and board to help test the key assumptions and anticipate the various scenarios as to what might happen.

I noted that the planning process happens annually. That's actually only half true. As Yogi Berra once said, "In theory, there is no difference between theory and practice. In practice, there is." In practice, the financial plan is often reset midyear, because—as I mentioned earlier—a startup's budget is always wrong. To echo Donald Rumsfeld, there are just too many unknown unknowns. Therefore, by June, the company realizes that its actual performance compared to its budget is off the rails and requires a reforecast. The board then asks hard questions of the CEO: *What are the implications on cash consumption and when will we be out of cash? What are the implications to our P&L and how will it look to outside investors or prospective acquirers? What are the implications on sales and marketing efficiency and do we need to make adjustments as a result?* FP&A helps answer all of these questions. Between June and August, the financial plan is often reforecast, reset, reconfigured, and reissued to the board for a more accurate view as to how the rest of the year will play out. Everyone catches a breath for a few months, and then the planning cycle begins again in the fall.

THE BUDGET. Putting together a credible and achievable annual budget is much more valuable if you have established an underlying business plan for the company. In the first year or two of a startup, the long-term view is often encapsulated in the vision of the founding entrepreneur. This vision is typically a very high-level conceptual view of the kind of business she wants to build to solve a perceived problem in the market. However, once the business is up and running and once there are outside investors involved, it becomes important for the key stakeholders to establish a common view of the long-term strategic plan for the company. This plan should include a description and sizing of the market in which the company operates, an analysis of the company's strengths, weaknesses, opportunities, and threats (commonly known as a SWOT analysis), the key differentiators it seeks to establish vis-à-vis other players in the market, the long-term financial goals for the company, and the likely exit scenarios for the company. FP&A drives the creation of this longer-range financial plan (when I say *long*, I mean a three- to five-year time horizon—this is StartUpLand after all). The plan is ultimately manifested in the form of a budget. Some may think the tables of numbers in a budget are boring, but they tell a story about the company's priorities. I like to say that the budget is the strategy . . . and the strategy is the budget. In other words, what you spend money on represents your priorities.

CASH IS KING. The phrase "cash is king" is never more true than for startups. The most important model any start-up finance team can provide is a cash forecast—the more detailed, the better. It is imperative to know the drivers of cash usage and when working capital usage is most pronounced.

FP&A needs to build a medium-term (two- to three-year) model that answers the core question: *When do we run out of cash and need to raise more funds?* This model should also include assumptions about the cost of capital so you can have a view toward whether equity or debt would be a better source for capital when the company needs it.

When cash is particularly tight, you should also have a weekly or even daily cash forecast model so that the finance team can have tight controls over the inflow and outflow of cash. Nothing can kill a startup quicker than a lack of liquidity, and nothing can kill the morale of the employees faster than a concern over whether they are going to get paid.

WHAT MAKES A GOOD FP&A PERSON. Unlike controllers, FP&A folks do not necessarily have to come from accounting backgrounds. They can be former investment bankers, management consultants, or MBAs who have strong analytical skills and a knack for deconstructing business models. Although they may not necessarily need a CPA, they typically understand enough about GAAP to accurately produce and interpret financial statements.

More than years and years of experience, the most important characteristic in a good FP&A person is an insatiable curiosity. The right person for this role wants to know everything about the industry, the company, the product, and the functions within the company. The most critical question a competent FP&A person can ask is "Why?" While it is important to understand how the company is performing as compared to the annual budget or the prior year's results, it is far more important to understand why the variances (good or bad) have occurred. Revenue may be below plan, but *why*? Is it due to poor execution by the sales team? Or is it due to market-driven pricing compression as a result of increased competition? You can't address the problems of a startup if you don't know how to analyze them objectively and diagnose them precisely. Those are the key attributes of a strong FP&A executive.

KEY PERFORMANCE INDICATORS (KPIs). In addition to monitoring cash closely, each startup should identify three to five key performance indicators (KPIs) for each function that provide insight to the performance of that particular function. The FP&A team often work with the CEO to define those KPIs that have the largest impact on the business and then aggregate each of these KPIs into a set of operating KPIs that allow the management team to create a dashboard it can use to track the day-to-day health of the company. Each KPI should have a set of defined guardrails that identify the upper and lower level of "goodness" for that metric. Some startups like to color code their dashboards so that if the KPI is slightly out of bounds from the guardrails, it's considered "yellow" and if it's substantially out of bounds, it's "red." "Green" obviously means the KPI is within the appropriate bounds of goodness.

On a regular basis—at least monthly but weekly for some metrics—management should be reviewing these metrics to determine what their focus should be for that week or month.

Action plans with a distinct owner and deliverable should be established for any metric that falls outside the guardrails. Notice—I didn't limit the action plans to only those metrics that fall below the acceptable minimum. It is equally important for management to focus attention on KPIs that are performing better than what is deemed acceptable. Understanding what is causing a key metric to be better than expected and analyzing the root cause for the over-performance is as important as determining and eradicating root causes for underperforming KPIs.

To monitor these key performance indications, there is often, literally, a dashboard for the management team and board to review. At a startup, that dashboard might contain funnel metrics, such as app downloads, monthly active users (MAUs), and daily active users (DAUs). That dashboard might be operational in nature, showing metrics such as the number of customer service tickets opened, response times, and Net Promoter Score (NPS); or it may contain product development statistics, such as the number of bugs found and resolved and development tasks completed.

A MAYOR AND HIS KPIs. Let me give you an example of an effective dashboard—from the public sector, of all places, where one city mayor (like many institutions) is taking a page from the business practices of StartUpLand. In fact, I like this example for that very reason as it shows that many organizations—large and small, for-profit and not-for-profit—can benefit from the operating models developed in StartUpLand.

When Boston's Mayor Marty Walsh took office in 2014, he asked a young startup executive, Daniel Koh, to be his chief of staff. Like many of his friends, Koh had joined a startup early in his career—the news media pioneer, *Huffington Post*. After a few years there serving as the chief of staff to founder/CEO Arianna Huffington in a role that was similar functionally to FP&A (planning, analysis, business insight), he was lured into public service and hired as the mayor's chief of staff. In that role, he was asked to use his business skills to help make the mayor's office run more efficiently.

The mayor told Koh he wanted a visual dashboard like all the startup CEOs in Boston had, so Koh had a large, flat-screen monitor installed in the mayor's office. He and the mayor decided on all the metrics that mattered for the city's performance beyond its normal budget indicators—such as average time to fix a pothole, average time to get a permit approved, average call pickup time, and so on—and then he built a dashboard for the mayor's office.

Mayor Walsh used the dashboard to employ *management by observation*, or *management by visibility*, wherein what is visible gets managed. The mayor walks into the office and, if something is flashing red, he jumps on it. If he sees something out of bounds, he jumps on it. Figure 7-1 is an example chart from the mayor's dash board.

FIGURE 7-1

Sample City of Boston dashboard

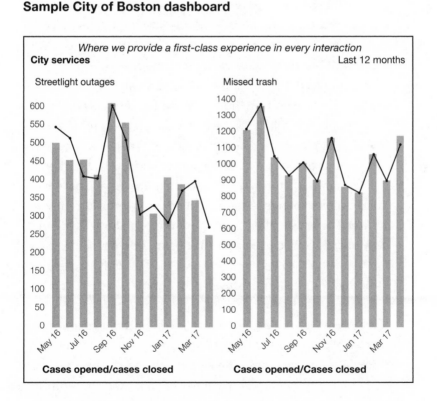

Source: City of Boston, www.cityofboston.gov/mayorsdashboard/.

Daniel Koh

Daniel Koh, Chief of Staff for Boston Mayor Marty Walsh

Boston is nearly a $3 billion operating budget organization. If it were in the private sector, it would be a *Fortune* 1000 company and deeply data driven. Yet, in the public sector, very few elected officials are using data to inform their decision making in the same way. We wanted to change that. We wanted to make sure the mayor had extensive data at his fingertips at all times, because we feel taxpayer dollars should be examined with the same scrutiny that shareholder dollars are. The goal was to get the entire administration thinking of data as a key factor in everyday decision making, and it has worked—streetlights are fixed faster, potholes filled more efficiently, and the decisions we make with our dollars are better informed.

We sought data for things we feel are key to the city's health—everything from homicide statistics to library visits. Though one will never be able to get a comprehensive measure of a city's performance through metrics alone, we feel the more relevant data we gather and study, the more of a complete picture we will have of the city and the way our citizens experience their local government. Currently, we track approximately thirty measures and have made our dashboards publicly available at boston.gov/cityscore.

The dashboard immediately had an incredibly positive effect on the way our staff worked. People were excited that they were able to measure and track their performance day to day. We were told of an employee in Veterans Services who was instructed to track how many calls were coming in from veterans each day. She was so excited by this that she was rallying her entire department to "beat the score" from the day before.

We designed a scoring system for our performance, called "CityScore." For each metric, we have a target and score ourselves each day as to how far above or below target we are for that metric. If we're below target, it shows up in red. The mayor each day immediately zeroes in on the red scores and will ask us to address it. Over the last few months, he noticed that our ambulance response times were in the red and asked us to look into it. We discovered that because our population was growing so fast, our response times were not as swift. As a result, we bought a new fleet of ambulances for the next fiscal year, and we've seen our response times improve. It is not hyperbole for us to say that we think CityScore has saved lives.

Business Operations

With the emergence of KPI dashboards, the finance function can now expand its measuring capabilities from traditional finance metrics to virtually any metric relevant to the business's core operations. This more recent phenomenon in StartUpLand has resulted in the creation of a business operations (Biz Ops) function, which involves the monitoring of a range of data and deriving business intelligence from it. Like Marketing Ops and Sales Ops (covered in chapters 4 and 6, respectively), the Biz Ops function has become a rising trend as startups are trying to take advantage of the wealth of data coming out of the various internal systems. This data needs to be collected, analyzed, and acted on. For many startups, the FP&A function already does this for financial data, but some companies are now creating this separate function charged with performing this role on operational data. Thus, Biz Ops turns data into useful reports and dashboards that executives can draw conclusions from and, based on these conclusions, make decisions.

The Biz Ops role varies widely depending on the startup's organization structure, but in all cases companies look to Biz Ops to be in the middle of the action—keeping a big-picture view of the business, analyzing the KPIs, and pushing the more creative or technical staff members at the startup to think like shareholders. In a startup organized by function, there may be a Biz Ops person assigned to each functional area. In a startup large enough to be organized by business unit, Biz Ops might be assigned to each business unit manager. In all cases, Biz Ops focuses on providing operational analysis and identifying potential areas of improvement.

Biz Ops sometimes overlaps a bit with Sales Ops and Marketing Ops. In a smaller company, those roles might be combined into one, often like a chief of staff who drives operational projects across the company. In a larger company, it is common for each function to have its own, assigned Biz Ops resource.

PROFILE

Tamara Zagorovskaya

Tamara Zagorovskaya, Business Operations and Strategy, Pinterest

Before joining Pinterest, I started my own company, which gave me real appreciation both for how challenging it is to succeed as an entrepreneur and how thrilling it is to delight a customer with a product that you built yourself.

In my current role, I'm responsible for revenue forecasting and strategic cross-functional projects. My group sits within the finance organization, reporting to the CFO, and plays a critical role in the planning process. I used to work for a private equity firm, where I built high-level financial models for late-stage companies across many industries, evaluating investments and working with portfolio companies on strategic alternatives. In my current role, the ultimate decision is not "Should we invest in this company?" Instead, it's "How do we grow the company?" A finance or consulting background is valuable in Biz Ops because the role requires taking broad questions (e.g., "Which international market should we launch next?") and distilling them into actionable frameworks and detailed financial models.

Since the business model at a startup is continuously evolving, the operating models that I build are used to evaluate strategic decisions. For example, how do we measure the success of a new product launch?

Furthermore, we have extensive data available to us, so I spend a lot of time extracting large data sets using SQL [structured query language, used to communicate with databases]. Given my role in driving strategic planning and analysis, which affects budgeting and cash flow management, my models are very granular and require me to work cross-functionally across the organization to get alignment on assumptions. I'm also constantly keeping a pulse on the health of the business by identifying key metrics and monitoring them via dashboards—this comprehensive understanding of the day-to-day drivers combined with a holistic view of the long-term trajectory is the unique perspective that Biz Ops provides to our executive team.

In startups, I've found that change is truly the only constant—at a fast-growing technology company, there is still room to influence the trajectory of the business, so my projects frequently change based on current business needs, and I am constantly reprioritizing how I spend my time. As the company grows, the structure of the organization inherently evolves, so there's no static org chart—you have to figure out who to talk to on your own. Being proactive in getting to know people in other parts of the org is especially important in Biz Ops because my projects often touch many other functional areas such as sales, marketing, and product.

I wanted to be at a mission-driven company that was making products or services that helped people learn new things. In terms of company size, I sought out a growth-stage company that had already achieved product/market fit so I could help the business scale while gaining exposure to a variety of functional areas and skills. I enjoy my current role because I get to influence strategy for an organization that is directly impacting the lives of people around the world. Plus, I am a passionate user of the product, so working on making the product and company better makes coming to work pretty fun.

Fundraising and Investor Relations

The final finance function that you will see in startups has to do with bringing the money in—fundraising—and then keeping in good touch with your investors—investor relations.

Because fundraising at a startup occurs every year or two, and because in a business, cash is akin to oxygen, founders frequently are required to focus on the fundraising process. As a company grows, the VP of Finance or CFO will assist the CEO in running the fundraising process. I have written a great deal about fundraising, dedicating an entire book to the subject called *Mastering the VC Game*, so I won't go into great detail here.[1] Instead, it is simply worth noting that many young entrepreneurs who do not yet have an experienced head of Finance will turn to a more junior professional to assist them in the fundraising process. The effort may be a special project for an outsider—for example, a former venture capital associate or investment banker—or perhaps a full-time role for a period of time (often labeled a "chief of staff" or "business development director," even though in fundraising, the main business being developed is financial capital).

The investor relations (IR) role becomes more relevant at a later-stage startup, typically in preparation for an IPO. The IR director is hired to work closely with the CEO and the marketing communications department to treat investors as customers, providing an interface with them and setting up all the necessary communication tools so that they are able to stay abreast of when and where company executives might be presenting at various industry conferences and answering questions about the quarterly financial reports and various industry news.

The Benefits of Startup Finance

As you can see, being a part of the finance team at a startup provides you with the opportunity to be a part of many of the company's most critical processes, from fundraising to sales to performance analysis. So early-stage finance professionals get to do a broad range of things, including:

- Selecting and implementing financial systems

- Creating the accounting framework from scratch

- Building first-ever business plans

- Developing and analyzing the company's business model

- Creating and maintaining budgets

- Raising capital

- Establishing policies and procedures

- And a lot more

Even if you're a junior finance person, there's a huge difference in the kinds of experiences you'll have in a startup versus a big company. In a big company, as an FP&A person, you may model an individual product launch or an individual business unit. In a startup, you'll model the entire company. You have to bring everything together and figure out when the company is running out of cash, when it needs to raise more money, what assumptions people are making about the global market, and what the sensitivities are on those assumptions.

In a startup, it's key to always think about the company view and to think about equity value creation at the top level. It's also important to be a holistic thinker, because you'll be thinking about the board of directors' perspective and the CEO's perspective on the company's financial situation.

You can't afford to take a narrow view when working in a startup, not even in Finance. You need to be a multiskilled athlete—a decathlete—with an opportunity to have a significant impact on a company's success.

RESOURCES

- *The Art of Startup Finance*, with Bill Reichert (video). https://www.entrepreneurship.org/learning-paths/the-art-of-startup-finance. The Kauffman Foundation, which is an amazing entrepreneurial advocacy and educational nonprofit, published a great video series. One of those videos is from veteran VC Bill Reichert discussing the art of startup finance, including analyzing your business model and budgeting.

8. **The Search Process**

As I noted in chapter 1, the startup universe is a large one and can seem overwhelming and impenetrable to the uninitiated. And that's why I'm often asked by freshly minted graduates and seasoned professionals alike how they should go about getting a job at a startup. They know that StartUpLand has all these magical, positive attributes, but they're afraid of it because they don't know how to break into it. Often they have functional experience; they may come from the marketing department at IBM, for example, or the product management department at Staples, or the finance department at GE. Yet, they do not know quite how to apply those functional skills into a startup role. Also, they may have trouble knowing how to find the right fit. I've had such conversations many, many times.

A few years ago, a mutual friend introduced me to someone who worked for eBay. At that time, eBay was already a big company with thousands and thousands of employees. This person was in the finance department there and was keen to translate his experience into a startup. He said, *I don't really know how to begin. I'm not sure I'm ready to be the CFO of a startup, but I think I could be helpful and effective somehow. I don't really know what I'm interested in.* So we had this conversation, and I went through my methodology, and he realized he was interested in e-commerce, and wanted to come to Boston for personal reasons and continue to leverage his experience in finance. After weeks of searching in a targeted fashion, he ended up in the finance department, doing business operations, at a small, Boston-based, early-stage e-commerce company. As the company grew, he got promoted to CFO. When the founder was fired a few years later, he got a battlefield promotion and became CEO and helped accelerate the company's growth. In a very short period of time, he had gone from being a middle manager in eBay's finance department to being the CEO of an exciting, venture-backed e-commerce startup.

Having had this conversation over and over again with talented professionals of all ages across all backgrounds has helped me build up a methodology. The methodology is straightforward and involves two simple things:

- Choose the best fit for you

- Position yourself well

This chapter takes a look at both.

Choosing the Best Fit for You

Having read this entire book and gotten a sense of the different roles and functions of a startup, you now presumably have a point of view regarding what job is the best fit for you. Now you need to choose the right startup to pursue that job. Selecting the right company fit has four steps:

- Pick a domain

- Pick a city

- Pick a stage

- Pick a winner

Here's what each step means and how to apply it.

Picking a Domain

First, figure out your passion with regard to domain. This means asking yourself a bunch of questions. It's like an optometrist's exam: Which is better? Lens A? Or B? C? Or D?

Start by asking, *Am I more of a B2C type or a B2B type? Serving the needs of large businesses or small businesses?*

Then ask, *What are my favorite three apps on my phone? What's my favorite product? What brand do I admire the most? What's my favorite online service? What's my favorite company?*

These questions can also force you to think very tangibly. For example, if you decide TripAdvisor is your favorite app, maybe it says something about a passion for travel, and maybe you should look for a startup in the travel sector.

Moving on from there, ask, *What blogs do I read? What articles in* TechCrunch *capture my attention?*

I like to do something I call the *Wall Street Journal* test, which is simply to ask: "When you're reading the *Wall Street Journal* (or *Bloomberg BusinessWeek* or *Fortune* or *Forbes*), what articles do you skip and what articles do you read thoroughly?" What you read is always a very telling signal of what you're intellectually interested in. If you find yourself skipping past headlines of articles about, say, the media business, then you probably shouldn't join a new media startup. If you find yourself diving into things written about autonomous vehicles, or are really interested in mobile gaming, obsessed with the latest articles about Pokemon Go and about virtual and augmented reality, then the startups that touch those areas are the ones you should pursue and dig into.

In the world of B2C, maybe you're more interested in something like e-commerce or online services or media, either global or national. If you land on global B2C e-commerce, then you can start considering the kinds of companies that fit into that bucket.

If you decide that you're really interested in food rather than consumer products, then you focus in that direction. For example, there is a ton of innovation going on in food tech and delivery, as well as healthy lifestyle and Millennial-focused food brands. However, if you're really interested in how technology is disrupting the healthcare industry, then you should focus on that. Then, try to narrow things down further, depending on whether you are more fascinated by healthcare IT, healthcare services, medical devices, diagnostics, biopharma, or genomics.

Answering these questions will help narrow your focus down to a set of domains that you are excited about. You can land on more than one, but you shouldn't end up with more than three; otherwise, your search will become too broad and unfocused. An easy way to irritate the network of friends poised to help you enter StartUpLand is by saying, "I don't know what I'm interested in." The landscape is too broad to be helpful to someone taking this approach.

Picking a City

Next, figure out where you want to live.

If you don't already live in a startup hub, I very highly recommend moving to one—not only for the job you are about to take now, but because it means you'll be in the right place for the next *several* jobs. Wherever you work, you're going to meet other people, whether at the company you join or in the community at large, and they are going to be your future colleagues for the next startup, and the next startup, and the one after that. Every startup hub has its own culture, and you should assume that one job will lead to another. If you make the move to join a startup in a particular city, you will connect with a network of people that you are going to continue to want to work with in multiple companies over multiple years. So pick that city wisely in the context of your personal fit with the community and its values and lifestyle, whether it's because family is nearby, or your spouse found a job there, or because it's a city you're excited to live in for personal reasons. The best situation, and the most frequent one, is that whatever company you work for, you end up leveraging and building on a strong network of people, company after company.

Focusing on a location that is not a startup hub can limit your opportunities. (Some companies and people are willing to work remotely, with occasional travel, but this will still leave you limited with regard to future jobs and in becoming part of the community in that city.) It's simple: if you're geographically inhibited or cut off, you may just have to move. The wrong location can really reduce your odds of success.

For some, the conventional wisdom is that the only startup hub in the world that matters is Silicon Valley (an area that, when talking about startups, refers to the fifty-mile stretch from San Jose to San Francisco and the surrounding area). What Broadway is to musical theatre and Hollywood is to movies, Silicon Valley is to StartUpLand.

Although Silicon Valley is far and away the largest startup hub— attracting the most amount of capital and some of the most talented startup leaders in the world—there are other high-quality areas worthy of consideration when it comes to joining StartUpLand. Other top-tier US startup hubs include Boston, Los Angeles, and New York. Other smaller but still vibrant startup hubs are Boulder (Colorado), Chicago, and Seattle. Internationally, you might consider London or Berlin in Europe; Tel Aviv, Bangalore, or Shanghai in Asia; or São Paulo or Buenos Aires in South America. Whatever geography you choose, be intentional and strategic. Startup ecosystems are tight communities with distinct characteristics, centered around the local universities, large technology companies in the area, high-profile venture capitalists, and successful entrepreneurs.

Some factors to consider when selecting geography:

- Pick a city that has a cluster of companies in the field you're interested in. That way, if your startup happens to fail, you have other companies in related fields that could be a fit. New York City is a hotbed of fashion tech companies, for example. If the first one you join doesn't work out, your experience will still be highly valued at the next one.

- If your spouse needs to work, pick a city with opportunities for him or her as well. Many startup executives I know end up in Boston because their spouses are in the medical field.

- Pick a city whose weather and lifestyle is appealing to you. For example, if you love the beach, it's hard to beat joining a startup in Santa Monica. If you're a passionate skier, Boulder may be worthy of consideration. And if you hate snow, you're not going to want to move to Boston (as much as I love it!).

Again, there may be multiple options, but ideally you should pick one or two favorites. Each startup community has its own pros and cons, quirks, and vibe.

Here's why picking the right geography is so important: once most people choose a particular startup community, they tend to settle in and stay there. It's a natural phenomenon—they build relationships over time that lead from one opportunity to another. Your coworkers in one startup could become your cofounders in another. So in thinking about geography, think about playing chess, not checkers. Think three to four professional moves ahead and whether you want to remain in that geography throughout each of those moves.

Picking a Stage

The next step in figuring out how to pursue opportunities at startups is to determine what stage company you prefer to work in.

In chapter 1, I shared the framework I like to use of the three stages of a startup: jungle, dirt road, and highway. The decision regarding which of these three stages is right for you should be made somewhat based on your appetite for risk, and somewhat on your personal makeup and preferences. If you are a risk-taker and enjoy the challenges and roller-coaster ride, then the jungle phase is for you, and you should bias toward seed-funded or recently Series A–funded companies that are pre-revenue and have not yet achieved product/market fit. If you are more conservative, want a good salary, and prefer to pick a "safe" winner, then a highway-phase company that is post–product/market fit and either pre-IPO or recently IPO'ed is the right choice.

It's about the degree of uncertainty—the amount of chaos—you're comfortable with. In the jungle stage, you're a figure-it-out person. In a dirt-road stage, it's already been mostly figured out for you, and now you're trying to scale and systematize it. In the highway stage, it's more about incremental improvement and continuous operation. Are you a figure-it-out person, or are you a systems builder? Do you like a lot of dynamism, or do you prefer steady, stable, continuous improvement and continuous operation?

I know many professionals new to StartUpLand who want to ease into it by joining a larger firm so that they have some structure and support around them. Then, after a few years of getting comfortable in the work environment and learning from those around them, they feel they can take more risk and join an earlier-stage firm. Others who join a small firm swear to me that their learning is more accelerated than their peers at larger startups. They are forced to take on more responsibility and are exposed to a broader set of roles and responsibilities as opposed to getting buried in an organizational silo. Even if the startup fails, they feel they are better positioned to be an effective leader in the next one.

The stage you prefer may also depend on your functional focus. For example, if you are interested in product management, then the earliest days may be a fit for you. Before a startup finds product/market fit, the product organization has a lot of the power, and Product and Engineering have a lot of the company's head count. After the company finds product/market fit, Sales and Marketing grow in both head count and power, and the product organization becomes more focused on incremental improvements.

Another consideration is the potential for financial gain.

I've talked several times in this book already about the job growth and impact potential you can have in StartUpLand. The other reward side is the equity. Joining a startup during the early stage—the jungle stage—usually gives you ten times the equity than you'll get when joining at the dirt-road stage. The same job during the highway stage may offer just one-tenth of the equity you'd get at the dirt-road stage. It's a huge difference.

It depends on your priorities. If your priorities are about putting your kid into a good school district and not having to move for the next five years, there might be more personal rewards in a more stable company than one in the jungle stage. You may not have to work quite so hard. You may have more stability. There will be a lower risk of ending up with a failed company on your resume later on. But if you like the jungle stage and you can stomach the risk of being part of a company in the midst of this dynamic stage, then such a choice can be very lucrative and rewarding.

Picking a Winner

This piece of advice is the hardest one to execute. All of the other steps are very objective measures—the stage of the company, the city, the domain. Picking a winner (i.e., a company that you think will be a massive success in the marketplace and therefore provide you with tremendous growth opportunities) is a subjective exercise. It's rife with mistakes. Even the best, most brilliant, and most experienced investors in the world are wrong over half the time. And while they have the benefit of holding a portfolio of companies, you only get to pick one to work for.

In selecting a startup to join, you ideally want to be part of a hot, dynamic company that has great momentum and potential.

How does an outsider figure out who are the likely winners in a given domain, market and stage? One way is to ask a handful of insiders. Find the top three VCs, angels, startup lawyers, and headhunters in your target geographical market and ask them to name the three hottest companies that match the domain and stage you are interested in (and then the bonus follow-up question: *Will you introduce me?*). Compile this list, pressure-test it, and see what patterns you find. The startups with the most compelling underlying evidence of success and momentum will naturally rise to the top.

Obviously, in the end, you should apply your own judgment based on your assessment of the company and its team. Do your own due diligence, and don't be afraid to be cynical about the spin you hear about a particular startup in the media versus the reality inside the four walls. How does an outsider conduct due diligence like an insider? Use the rubric that all investors use. Evaluate each company along the same criteria we venture capitalists employ, which are typically three simple ones:

- *Team:* Is the founding team compelling? Can they articulate a vision that inspires you and others around them? Are they of high integrity? Would you want to work with them again in their next company?

- *Market:* Is the market that the company is operating in massive (i.e., greater than $1 billion in revenue potential)? Is the market experiencing some kind of disruption that might lead to opportunity for a new entrant like this startup? How crowded is the market, and does this startup have a sustainable unfair advantage over the competition?

- *Business model:* Are the unit economics (i.e., the comparison of revenues and costs of each customer unit or product unit) attractive? Is the company already able to articulate the lifetime value of each customer, the acquisition cost of each customer, and compare the two? Does the company's business model contain network effects—that is, will the business get more valuable as the network of users grows such that initial market momentum will result in more momentum and value? If it has customers, do they appear loyal and have growth potential over time or are they canceling the relationship (churning out)?

You can pose these questions directly to the management team of the startups as well as yourself based on what you can see. And ask these questions of people who you believe have good judgment across multiple startups who can share their perspectives with you. The best people to ask are going to be people already in the industry you're looking at. If you already know some people in that industry, reach out to them to ask these questions. This process will help you narrow down a potentially paralyzing sea of options to a much smaller starting point. If you don't already know people in that industry, the next section—on positioning yourself—can help you find some.

As discussed, picking a winner is hard for professional investors like me. Thus, do not expect to pick the next Facebook or Google on every try. You will want to blend your best survey of conventional wisdom with your own judgment and instincts. Even if you are wrong (worst case, if the company you join fails), you can point to a thoughtful methodology when the next interviewer asks you "Why did you join that company and what did you learn from it?"

Note, too, that there is often a trade-off to consider when you're trying to select a winner. An earlier-stage company, particularly one that is not necessarily perceived as "hot" and has a huge amount of momentum, will be more willing to take a risk on you and give you more responsibility than a more mature growth stage company. At the earlier stages, you will have the opportunity to play multiple roles, grow more rapidly, and have more senior exposure. The downside is that you are less likely to have great mentors from whom you can learn as compared to a larger startup. Further, it is more likely that this early-stage startup will fail or go sideways and you will be looking for another job in a year or two. If you are willing to take more risk and operate with greater uncertainty, the quality of the experience at the early-stage startup can be superior to that of being a small cog in the larger, hot startup.

This series of steps—picking your domain, your city, the stage you're most interested in, and companies within that city that fit that stage in that sector—generally results in a very small list. Thus, at that point, you can decide which companies to focus on. If you're in a larger startup community—like San Francisco, New York, or Boston—you tend to have a lot of companies that are in the particular stage and sector.

Once this heuristic is complete, you have your target list.

Positioning Yourself Well

Once you have your target list, the next challenge is to try to position yourself well so that the startups would actually want to hire you. The two most important things you can do toward this goal are:

- Navigate your way to a warm introduction.

- Be prepared, once you walk into the room, to have a point of view about the company and what you can do to be helpful to them.

Getting a Warm Introduction

If you can't navigate your way to a warm introduction (i.e., a connection through a mutual acquaintance) at one of these startups, you're already demonstrating that you lack strong networking skills, which is a minus. All of these companies are full of people with big social media presences, big networks, and very transparent online footprints. Even the companies at very early stages, with thin or nonexistent websites, tend to have information about them on Crunchbase or on Mattermark, which list executives and investors and how much money they have raised. You can search for them on LinkedIn and see who their early employees are. Through those various networks and databases, you should be able to identify the key people and find a way to some warm introductions. Maybe it takes two degrees of separation, but you can try to connect to one person who can connect you to the next.

Let's say a woman named Sandra works at Codecademy, which is an online school in New York City trying to teach the world to code. And let's say you've decided that you want to get into education technology, and you live in New York City, and you've heard that Codecademy is a hot company.

You need to find a way to get to someone at Codecademy. If you don't know already know Sandra, and if you don't already know an executive at Codecademy or a staff member at Codecademy, you have to find somebody who knows Sandra. She may not be the hiring manager per se, but you need to get to somebody who can give you insight into the company and help you get to the hiring manager.

LinkedIn is a very useful tool in that regard. You can search for Sandra by name or search for Codecademy and immediately see how many degrees of separation you are from somebody who works there. If you are two degrees of separation, that means you know somebody who knows Sandra. The two of you have a mutual friend. Let's call him Jason. You can call him up and say, *Hey Jason, I'm really fired up about education technology and working for Codecademy would be a dream job. I think you are friends with Sandra, who works there.* Then, with luck, Jason says, *Yes, I know Sandra. We went to college together. She's great. I'm happy to make the introduction.*

Boom. You've got a mutual friend who can introduce you to Sandra.

But don't just ask Jason to shoot out a quick email. Ask Jason, when making this introduction, to make sure he tells Sandra that you're a great person, and why he thinks Codecademy would be lucky to have you. Basically, you ask Jason to give you a bit of an endorsement.

That's a warm introduction.

Assuming Jason and Sandra have a close connection, she will always be responsive to that sort of an inquiry. If you left a cold voicemail for Sandra, the stranger, this would go nowhere. But if your old buddy Jason connects you, Sandra will take the introduction much more seriously than she would a voicemail from a stranger. You can then meet Sandra (face-to-face is always best, so come up with a reason to make sure that happens!) and tell her you're interested in jobs at Codecademy.

Venture capitalists and angel investors are a great channel as well, if you happen to know any. They are often happy to pass along your resume and background to their portfolio companies.

After all, the companies in their portfolios always need qualified talent, and they feel it is their job to help their companies hire great people at all levels of the organization.

Before talking to a startup, make sure you have your own personal story straight. Startup Institute, a vocational training program, advises its students to think through their personal motivations, strengths, skills, and experiences and to weave a career narrative that helps infuse the networking process with focus. When introducing yourself to those in the community who can help you with introductions, thinking through and crafting your career narrative provides the proper account as to why you want to connect with that particular startup and how you can help them. Remember, startup hiring is not an impersonal matching process of skills to job requirements. From the startup's point of view, it is investing its precious resources in you and the potential of who you can become and how you can impact its growth and value.

Notice that I have yet to mention recruiters—headhunters—anywhere in the discussion about networking your way to companies. Recruiters can be an excellent source of intelligence because they know who's hiring, but I wouldn't spend a lot of time or energy working with one as you seek to enter StartUpLand. Recruiters are often more focused on executive hires than midlevel hires. If you're a senior executive looking for a CFO job or a VP Marketing job, they can be helpful. But in most cases, positioning yourself and earning a warm introduction from an insider can get you far more success.

In general, the startup community is incredibly generous with its time and has such a strong "pay it forward" culture, that with tenacity and time you can get to almost anyone.

In fact, I recommend you aim high. Use the heuristics I've described in this chapter to narrow down your search and then list out ten people who would be your absolute top choices to sit down with for thirty minutes face-to-face for networking purposes. Then go after those ten people in any way you can (granted, without stalking them or being a nudge). Even if it turns out the job fit isn't right, networking meetings like this will help you establish valuable relationships and will lead to additional, interesting meetings and connections.

In short, be organized, focused, and tenacious. Aim high, seek out the incremental networking meetings, and pick yourself out a prospective winner. Things may not work out, but at least you're putting yourself in a position for a little positive serendipity.

Have a Point of View about the Company and How You Can Contribute

Now for the second part of my advice: Be prepared to articulate how you can help the company you contact.

This means doing your research. Before you talk to Sandra, do your homework on Codecademy. Read everything you can online. Maybe even talk to a couple of the company's customers—a couple of friends who are using the service. Try out the service yourself. Take a bunch of notes about ideas for how to improve the product. If you're a designer, you may have specific ideas to make the product appear more attractive. If you're a marketer, you may have an idea for a new campaign or message. Sign up for the newsletters and try to see what the patterns are for their email campaigns. Then, when you meet Sandra, you can walk in and say, *It looks like you guys are really emphasizing your Pro product and executing well on the freemium model. I have some ideas as to how you could adjust the messaging for the product based on my experience at Procter & Gamble.*

Instead of merely pitching your work, engage with Sandra in conversation about *her* work. Sandra—I guarantee—is going to get off the phone or walk out of the coffee shop and think, *That was a great conversation with a great person!*

Yes, this all means doing a lot more work than, say, glancing at the "Careers" section of a startup's website and applying blindly, but it's a much stronger connection that has a much better chance of turning into something.

It's about standing out. If you only make it to the HR department's inbox, you're not going to stand out. On the other hand, if you network your way to relevant people, you can engage them in conversation, build relationships, get strong introductions from mutual friends, and thus jump to the top of the stack.

The other thing I recommend is to engage the principals of the company in content-rich dialogue. You can do that by attending conferences, company open houses, meetups, and other industry events where you know those principals are going to be. I admit it borders on stalker behavior, but it is effective if you handle it diplomatically.

Almost all startup CEOs and executives blog or are on social media. Engage with them through those channels by, for example, retweeting their tweets or commenting on their LinkedIn or Medium posts. If you see they are speaking at a conference, show up to chat with them after their panel. Put yourself into their flow. Get on their radar screen. Then, when you get the chance, talk to them about the work they're doing and how you've been studying their domain for the last two months and how you'd love to come in and swap observations.

It's strategic communication. It's intentional communication.

Finally—and this one is a bit of a secret weapon that few people do well—*come bearing gifts.*

When most people are looking for a job, they carry with them something to ask for. They enter a phone conversation or walk into a meeting focused on what they want: *I want an introduction, I want an interview, I want a callback, I want a job offer.*

If you flip that around so that instead you come bearing gifts, you have a completely different relationship. You come with advice. You come with connections. You can say, *Hey, Sandra, how can I help? Anything you need? What are you looking for? What are you challenged with? Oh, you need to hire a designer? Actually, I worked with a great designer in my last job, I can recommend a fantastic designer for you.* Come bearing gifts, and suddenly you'll be perceived as someone who is adding value.

I once heard about a product manager who had started at a mid-sized software company by working in the call center for several months. He took the entry-level job as a path into the company, but he then used all of his time in the call center talking to customers and getting valuable insights from them and writing them down and turning them into ideas. One day, he brought a massive stack of these ideas to the head of Product, dropped them on his desk, and said, *I want to do this*. Rather than ask for a job, he delivered value.

Who wouldn't hire that person?

As a result, in one step, he went from working in the call center as a tech support person to product management.

You could do the same thing even from the outside. With a B2C product, or even a B2B product, you can find customers who use the product and talk to them. Then, once you make your inside connection, you can come in with *ideas*.

———

If you secure a warm introduction, have a compelling narrative, engage in a content-rich dialogue, and come bearing gifts, you will deliver value. You create a two-way value exchange rather than a one-way set of requests. Don't be a supplicant looking for a handout.

Startup Compensation

After you have figured out your role, selected a startup that represents a good fit, and finally secured an offer to join, the next common question I get is: "How much should I be paid?" There's no one answer, of course, and the question is further complicated by the fact that startup compensation is typically a blend of cash compensation and equity compensation in the form of stock options.

Startup compensation is more of an art than a science. Because each company is young and immature, there may not be any clear compensation standards yet established. And compensation levels vary across startups, even when the role may be the same, because each startup is in a different situation in terms of capital raised and business maturity.

That said, there are a few guidelines that might help. As I've noted, startups fall into three typical stages of development: the jungle, the

TABLE 8-1

Typical ranges of cash and stock option compensation

	Jungle	Dirt road	Highway
Executive team (C-suite)			
Compensation	$150,000–$200,000	$175,000–$225,000	$200,000–$250,000
Stock option	1.0–2.0%	0.75–1.50%	0.50–0.75%
Vice president			
Compensation	$125,000–$150,000	$150,000–$200,000	$175,000–$225,000
Stock option	0.50–1.0%	0.25–0.75%	0.10–0.50%
Director			
Compensation	$80,000–$110,000	$100,000–$150,000	$125,000–$175,000
Stock option	0.20–0.50%	0.10–0.30%	0.05–0.20%
Manager			
Compensation	$60,000–$100,000	$75,000–$125,000	$75,000–$125,000
Stock option	0.05–0.20%	0.03–0.10%	0.02–0.05%

dirt road, and the highway. Table 8-1 provides the ranges of cash and stock option compensation that you might typically see at a startup at each stage based on the role you are being hired in to.

The value of startup stock options is difficult to interpret. They represent a contract between the company and the employee that gives the employee the right to purchase stock at a specific price (the *strike price*) if they so choose (*exercising the option*). Thus, when a company talks about how many shares it has outstanding, it typically refers to the number of shares the founders own plus the shares the company has sold to investors plus the number of options issued to employees plus the number of shares set aside for future employees (referred to as the *stock option pool* or the *unissued pool* because these options have not yet been issued). This total is known as the number of *fully diluted* shares outstanding.

The option figures shown in table 8-1 represent the percentage of the fully diluted shares in the company you are issued. To take a simple example, if you have 1,000 stock options and the company has a total of 100,000 fully diluted shares outstanding, then you own 1 percent of the company. Or do you?

More accurately, you have the option to buy enough shares of stock to own 1 percent of the company, and those options have a price—the strike price. Let's say your strike price is $1 per share. Then to exercise all of your options and own 1 percent of the company, it costs you $1,000. If the company is acquired by another company for $10 million in cash, and thus each share is acquired for $100, you net $99 per share or $99,000. Not quite 1 percent of the purchase price, but pretty close. If the difference between the company's sale price per share is closer to the strike price, the cost to acquire your shares is relatively higher, and thus your net proceeds relatively lower.

Every time a company raises money, it sells shares at a certain price. The price of those shares impacts the strike price of the options issued. Options can be issued at a discount to the investor price because investors get other rights and privileges for their shares they are paying for (e.g., certain controls and/or economic elements like dividends). So if a company is selling shares to investors at $4 per share, it may issue options to employees with a strike price that is half of that, or $2 per share.

These nuances are important when assessing offers from different startups. When asked for advice as to how to value the stock options, I encourage folks to set up a simple spreadsheet that lays out a few valuation scenarios (e.g., what if the startup were to eventually be acquired for $10 million, $50 million, $100 million?) and calculate the value of the stock options under each scenario based on the strike price and the ownership percentage, factoring in further dilution if the startup is not profitable and thus will need to raise money between now and exit. Then, assign probabilities to each of the valuation scenarios and multiply out the value of each scenario times the probability and sum those figures up to get an expected value. Don't forget to assign some probability that the company (and therefore your stock options) are worth zero. Usually, that's a big probability, so assign at least 50 percent, if not more!

Table 8-2 gives an example of this sort of scenario planning for the hypothetical option package of 1,000 stock options, representing 1 percent of the company fully diluted, at a $5 strike price.

TABLE 8-2

Scenario planning for evaluating stock option value

		COMPANY VALUE		
	$0	$10 million	$50 million	$100 million
Value per share	$0	$100	$500	$1,000
Net value of 1,000 options	$0	$95,000	$495,000	$995,000
Probability	50%	25%	15%	10%
Expected value	$0	$23,750	$74,250	$99,500

Sum of expected values weighted by probability: ($0 × 50%) + ($23,750 × 25%) + ($74,250 × 15%) + ($99,500 × 10%) = $27,025

Sum up these four expected values in the context of the probability weightings and you get $27,025. Thus, in your judgment, owning 1 percent of the company has an expected value of just under $30,000. This exercise can be helpful in mapping out how much you think the stock options are truly worth—both the range of possible values and the likelihood of hitting those values—and assist you in trying to normalize the value of an offer from one company as compared to another.

Specific Advice to Grads

Around graduation time each year, a lot of students start focusing on finding a job in StartUpLand and launching their careers. Few undergraduates and graduate students know how to get plugged in to the startup community and thus struggle with where to begin and what companies to target. You may have the same issue. The best startups may not be household names, and information about who's hot and who's not may seem to be hard to come by.

For many years, I have been keeping an updated list of interesting, scaling startups that are well regarded and are actively hiring (privately or publicly), organized by geography. I share this with the students in my class each spring to point them in the direction of high-quality, fast-growing companies worth exploring.

This is my own imperfect point of view with imperfect data (also combined with a sprinkling of data from market research firms Mattermark and CB Insights), but it might be useful for some candidates. You can find the current version on my blog at www.SeeingBothSides.com. The blog post is entitled "Advice to Grads: Join a Winning Startup," so just search for "winning."

Venture capitalist and professor Andy Rachleff of Stanford, cofounder of Wealthfront, does the same each fall, calling his the "Career-Launching Companies List," although his list is very San Francisco–based (over 60 percent of the startups he lists are in the Bay Area).

Conclusion

I hope this book has given you a sense of what startup life is like and how it can be most fulfilling for you. And hopefully, it provides a roadmap for how to find and get those jobs. Beyond all this, it's a matter of you doing your work, doing your research, and then going after that goal.

I should warn you: Almost nobody goes back the other way. A lot of people go from big companies to startups, while almost nobody who got bitten by the startup bug goes back to a big company. If they do, it's usually only to rebuild skills or networks or gain some additional credibility so they can get back into the startup world.

I find that people who work at startups are categorically happier with their jobs and with their careers than people who don't. Startups provide a greater degree of freedom and autonomy. There's the promise of a sense of mastery that people seem to really enjoy. And there's a sense of purpose—a really clear sense of purpose—because your actions are linked directly to the ups and downs of the company. In a big company, it's very hard to know how and what you should do to impact the greater whole. Yet, these are the key elements to happiness. And I think they're much more prevalent in startups than in other kinds of companies.

And in StartUpLand, you can always find something you're passionate about. Out there somewhere, there is always a startup that is a fit for your passion.

I've found all those things to be true in my own career. I was given an enormous amount of responsibility at a young age. I was totally over my head at almost every job I took on during my startup career, and I got promoted faster than I was prepared to be. It challenged me. It pushed me to step up my game every year. Just like with dog years, every one year of "startup time," as I like to call it, is like seven years at a regular company in terms of growth and responsibility, maturity, and growth.

Moreover, StartUpLand also gave me a great sense of purpose. I feel like all the jobs that I've been in have had a really clear sense of purpose—how what I'm doing fits into not only the company but the greater fabric. At Open Market, for example, we were working to make the internet safe for businesses. Thus, we were able to play a small role in the evolution of the internet. At Upromise, we helped millions of people save money for college and pursue their dreams.

To help people in some small way, whether it's by saving a little bit more or making their lives a little easier, is incredibly fulfilling. Everything I did was tied closely to those missions, the larger purposes. In a big company, I'm not sure I would have had that same sense. Accumulate all those roles at small companies that help advance innovation and technology and it can add up to having extraordinary impact on the world.

Now get out there and go for it. We can share that bottle of Dom when you come by my office to celebrate.

Notes

Chapter 1

1. *Wikipedia*, s.v. "Bussgang theorem," last modified December 6, 2016, https://en.wikipedia.org/wiki/Bussgang_theorem.

2. *Seeing Both Sides Blog*, "Why You Should Eliminate Titles at Startups," blog entry by Jeffrey Bussgang, July 13, 2011, https://seeing-bothsides.com/2011/07/13/why-you-should-eliminate-titles-at-start-ups/.

Chapter 2

1. Eric von Hippel, "Lead Users: A Source of Novel Product Concepts," *Management Science* 32, no. 7 (1986): 791–806.

2. Frederick P. Brooks, *The Mythical Man: Essays on Software Engineering* (Boston: Addison-Wesley, 1976).

3. Fareed Zakaria, *In Defense of a Liberal Education* (New York: W. W. Norton & Company, 2016).

Chapter 3

1. Thomas R. Eisenmann, Michael Pao, and Lauren Barley, "Dropbox: 'It Just Works'" (Boston: Harvard Business School Case 811-065, revised October 2014).

2. Thomas R. Eisenmann and Alison Berkley Wagonfeld, "Steven Carpenter at Cake Financial" (Boston: Harvard Business School Case 811-041, revised November 2014).

3. Pmarchive, "Part 5: The Moby Dick Theory of Big Companies," blog post by Marc Andreesen, June 27, 2007, http://pmarchive.com/guide_to_startups_part5.html.

4. *Hazard Lights Blog*, "Driving Developer Adoption," blog post by Chip Hazard, March 2, 2012, http://hazard.typepad.com/hazard-lights/2012/03/developer-driven-business-models.html.

Chapter 4

1. Gartner for Marketers, "Yes, CMOs Will Likely Spend More on Technology Than CIOs by 2017," blog post by Jake Sorofman, September 20, 2016, http://blogs.gartner.com/jake-sorofman/yes-cmos-will-likely-spend-more-on-technology-than-cios-by-2017/.

Chapter 5

1. *Paul Graham Blog*, "Startup = Growth," blog post by Paul Graham, September 2012, http://www.paulgraham.com/growth.html.
2. Kissmetrics, "Facebook's VP of Growth Gives You Tips on Growing Your Product," blog post by Zach Bulygo, https://blog.kissmetrics.com/alex-schultz-growth/.

Chapter 7

1. Jeffrey Bussgang, *Mastering the VC Game: A Venture Capital Insider Reveals How to Get from Start-up to IPO on Your Terms* (New York: Portfolio, 2011).

Index

Acknowledgments

This book would not have been possible without the support and guidance of my partners, David Aronoff, Kate Castle, Chip Hazard, and Jesse Middleton, to whom I am forever indebted. They continue to instruct and inspire me to figure out the secrets of StartUpLand. My work at Harvard Business School has put me in contact with hundreds of students who wish to enter StartUpLand, and as much as they may learn from me, I learn a tremendous amount from them. My journey at Harvard has been enriched with the wisdom of my colleagues in the entrepreneurship department, but particularly Lynda Applegate, who somehow persuaded me to join the faculty despite holding down a full-time job as a venture capitalist, and Tom Eisenmann and Jeffrey Rayport, with whom I've had the pleasure of teaching our course, Launching Technology Ventures.

Writing a book is hard work, and there have been many who helped me get started with some of the pieces. Those include Tom Eisenmann (again) and Rob Go on product management, Nadav Benbarak on growth, and Sarah Dillard, Katharine Nevins, Puja Ramani, and Tom Eisenmann (again) on business development, as well as Robert Hoekman throughout. Robert deserves special credit for helping me get my thoughts down in a clear, concise way through his many hours of dialogue and shrewd questions.

Others I'm indebted to include the amazing team at Harvard Business Review Press. Starting with Editorial Director Tim Sullivan and continuing throughout the organization—including Group Publisher Josh Macht, Julie Devoll, Stephani Finks, Jen

Waring, and Kenzie Travers—they have been extraordinarily efficient, professional, and supportive every step of the way.

I am similarly indebted to all who allowed me to interview them and include their stories and profiles. For this book I felt it important that all the profiles be of accessible, relatable people, and I'm grateful to all of them for opening up so candidly and humbly about their professional journeys.

In addition to my partners and other Flybridge team members (Jessica Buss, Matt Guiney, Bruce Revzin, and Kendall Sherman), I received amazing and insightful feedback from a host of reviewers, including Sparsh Agarwal, Sasanka Atapattu, Adria Brown, Frank Cespedes, Ellen Chisa, Ellen DaSilva, Tom Doctoroff, Tom Eisenmann, Stephanie Farris, Brad Feld, Ben Foster, Jodi Gernon, Meghan Gill, Oliver Jay, Alex Laats, Mitch Weiss, and Andrew Wilkinson. Thanks to each of you for your time and your contributions. I am blessed to have two highly supportive and editorially gifted parents, who painstakingly reviewed each chapter and helped me reduce the jargon.

Finally, I must acknowledge with great appreciation my wife and life partner, Lynda Doctoroff Bussgang. She helps me stay balanced and grounded and somehow—for nearly thirty years now—continues to humor me when I turn to her and say, "Honey, I have an idea . . . " I am incredibly blessed to have met her that first day freshman year.

About the Author

JEFFREY BUSSGANG is a venture capitalist, entrepreneur, and entrepreneurship professor at Harvard Business School (HBS). His firm, Flybridge Capital Partners, has over $600 million under management and has made investments in over one hundred technology-focused startups since inception over fifteen years ago. At HBS, he teaches Launching Technology Ventures, a popular class for MBA students starting companies or pursuing careers in start-ups. Before cofounding Flybridge, Bussgang was an entrepreneur—serving as cofounder and president of Upromise (acquired by Sallie Mae) and an executive team member at Open Market (IPO 1996). He is the author of *Mastering the VC Game*, an essential guide for entrepreneurs raising capital and building their startups, and over twenty HBS case studies, teaching notes, and book chapters regarding startup management and entrepreneurship. He started his career with The Boston Consulting Group and holds an MBA from HBS and a BA in computer science from Harvard College.